Sussex, Kent & Surrey 1939

By

RICHARD WYNDHAM

Illustrated from the Author's Photographs

BATSFORD

This edition first published in the United Kingdom in 2019 by
Batsford
43 Great Ormond Street
London WC1N 3HZ

An imprint of Pavilion Books Company Ltd

This book first published as *Last Look Round* (Batsford, 1940)

ISBN: 9781849945486

A CIP catalogue record for this book is available from the
British Library.

25 24 23 22 21 20 19
10 9 8 7 6 5 4 3 2 1

Repro by Mission Productions, Hong Kong
Printed by 1010 Printing International Ltd, China

This book can be ordered direct from the publisher at the website:
www.pavilionbooks.com, or try your local bookshop.

TO

THE ARM-CHAIR TRAVELLERS
OF THE SECOND GREAT WAR

PUBLISHERS' NOTE

THIS book was almost completed on the outbreak of the war, when the author was called up on active service. Under the circumstances it was impossible for him to complete certain districts, particularly Surrey, as comprehensively as he would have liked, or to make a final check-up on certain references and anecdotes. It was also thought best not to attempt to revise the book in view of recent events, but rather to leave it as it is—a nostalgic memory of England in the last months of peace.

November 1939

PREFACE

THIS is a travel-book rather than a guide-book. I have travelled at haphazard through South-Eastern England; but, for the most part, on side roads only, and through villages and lesser towns. In so short a book it seemed impossible to deal fully with " tourists' Meccas " such as Canterbury, Maidstone, Brighton or Chichester. And the London suburbs would have required a psychological treatise of length. Even with these omissions, my task appeared absurd until I discovered that, while my notes about certain places occupied several pages, about others they remained mere notes. The latter I discarded, and in consequence there must appear an inequality, which is the inequality of my own mind.

In search of my facts, I have picked too many brains to thank the owners individually—except Murray; and in acknowledging a special debt to his *Handbooks* I am surely voicing the gratitude of most English guide-book authors for nearly a century.

Private houses which are open to the public presented a problem that could only be solved by their omission. To have dealt with them all was impossible; to have selected or criticised would have been an abuse of hospitality.

R. W.

TICKERAGE MILL
August 23, 1939

INTRODUCTION

ONE cold Easter I was writing about the Romney Marsh in Kent, imagining I was out on the windswept pastures and in particular sitting in the white-painted box pews of the tiny church of Fairfield, which sits completely alone two miles south of Appledore. Surrounded by the Marsh sheep and reed-bordered dykes, this is a favourite location with film-makers for its remoteness and atmosphere. I wanted to see how other writers had described this church that served no village but still acted as a focal point for the surrounding farms and cottages. John Newman called it a 'diminutive, dumpy church set down pat on the marshes', Richard Ingrams thought it looked like 'a Noah's Ark that has come to rest' and Simon Jenkins had it 'deposited by the tide'. It was then that I reached for a book long collected but never read, perhaps subconsciously thinking the title suggested a county council draft plan. It appeared in the Batsford series *The Face of Britain: South-Eastern Survey* by Richard Wyndham. His Fairfield 'looks like a toy dropped by a child'. I quickly turned to the front of the book and as a result of this playfully apt description, read it cover to cover over what remained of Easter. When I finished I sat and marvelled that this eccentric, eclectic, wry and wonderful tour through the south eastern counties of England, just before the Second World War, had appeared to have been lost in the mists of the eighty years since 1939. It appeared as *South East England* in 1951 but was needlessly edited. What we see here is the original.

Guy Richard Charles Wyndham was born into the aristocracy in 1896, a descendant of George Wyndham, the third Earl of Egremont who lived at Petworth House in West Sussex. Dick Wyndham, as he was known, was brought up in a Philip Webb designed house, Clouds, in East Knoyle, Wiltshire, later left to him by a cousin. He was educated at Wellington College and at the Royal Military College at Sandhurst and subsequently won the Military Cross in the First World War. In 1927, despite having considerable wealth, he continued his habit of selling a family painting once a year 'to keep buoyant' and sold the 1899 painting of his three aunts (dubbed The Three Graces by the then Prince of Wales) by John Singer Sargent, for £20,000, to the Metropolitan Museum of Art in New York. Around this time he discovered on a walk, and subsequently bought, Tickerage Mill near Uckfield in East Sussex, a property later owned by actress Vivien Leigh. From here he wrote books, painted and made prints, and as Britain prepared for war was asked in 1939 by Batsford to write about his corner of England, a 'last look round' as he described it of Kent, Sussex, and Surrey. In the publisher's note you will see that it was almost completed when he was 'called up on active service'. (His daughter Joan, born in East Knoyle in 1927, came to prominence much later with her lively and romantic wartime diaries.) Wyndham was invalided out and became a foreign correspondent for the Sunday Times, but in a skirmish in Jerusalem between Israeli troops and the Arab League he was killed in 1948 by Israeli gunfire as he was taking a photograph of an Arab advance.

Brian Cook, later politician Brian Cook Batsford, illustrated many Batsford dust jackets. When the publisher came to initiating the series *The Face of Britain*, he hoped that the books would be planned around counties. But Harry Batsford insisted on geographical areas, such as the subsequent *Chiltern Country* and *Cotswold Country*. The new series was published alongside the very successful British Heritage books with their brilliantly-coloured jackets by Cook, but instead of the time-consuming Jean Berté printing process his illustrations for *The Face of Britain* were taken directly from his original paintings by photolithography. And so it was, as Richard Wyndham was finishing his writing and taking up arms, the cover for *South-Eastern Survey* was being painted. A farm labourer with his cap turned round stands on his empty wagon, giving the horse a rest as he looks over the landscape falling away from him. He sees a patchwork of fields, red-tiled roofs and the distant line of the Downs, whilst his workfellows are finishing loading a cart with hay.

Richard Wyndham wrote his book when already his beloved countryside was threatened by the increase of traffic on arterial roads and over development. The advent of affordable cars meant that Britain was now visited in places that hitherto could only have been reached by the railway, and the new guidebooks like those of Shell and indeed Batsford brought enticing views of British counties. The south east coast could be reached in a couple of hours from London, and Brighton was always an hour from Victoria. The topographical Batsford books of the 1930s almost always used photographs gained from outside sources, but *South Eastern Survey* exclusively used Wyndham's own images.

When one first opens the book and skims through the pictures, at first glance they may seem just like those in other Batsford books, but on closer inspection many of Wyndham's photographs are very different from anything else in a book of this type at this time. Although the scene probably courted his displeasure, he nevertheless found interest in Whitehawk Camp near Brighton with fences made from discarded iron bedsteads. The ruined farmhouse, sunrise gates and a single decker bus turned into a home in Leysdown on the Isle of Sheppey were unexpected images to see in a Batsford book. These are things some of us clamour to find now, and I wonder whether Richard Wyndham was the first to acknowledge them. He takes the trouble to take his photograph of oast houses in Kent by moonlight, and the backs, not fronts, of Bluecoat boys in Horsham. I suppose it's the painter's eye, seeing things the casual observer does not. He makes no comment on his photograph of a street in old Folkestone because the indecent plethora of signs says it all, or about the litter left by 'trippers' on Box Hill. I don't know what the make of car is whose bonnet stretches out in his shot of Saltdean, I don't know what camera he used, or what film, but he drove, walked and sat on trains to give us a unique account of the villages, towns and people that were soon to be on the home front line in the Second World War.

It's the writing though that really sets this book apart. All Batsford books were well-written by people who knew their subjects, but Richard Wyndham's personality seeps through onto the page to such an extent it make us glad that we are in his company. It is all too easy to see ourselves sitting next to him in a country inn as he talked with the locals, his fat sheepdog asleep under the table. Or to wish we were in the carriage with him on the Kent & East Sussex Railway as the trackside willow hedges brushed across the windows. If one incident serves not only to represent the uniqueness of this book, and shows us both just how much life has changed forever since 1939 and what we've irrevocably lost, then his account of the running of a country railway at Northiam station will serve us well.

For Wyndham this really was 'a last look round'; the chances are he never made these same journeys again, certainly not in the same spirit. So much has changed in Kent, Sussex and Surrey over eighty years that it might seem impossible to find the places as he did in 1939. Motorways slice up North Kent and Surrey, scarring the North Downs; the towns of Sussex expand under the roar of airliners climbing out over the Weald from Gatwick, the coastline becomes even more of a crowded playground. But what is remarkably still true is Wyndham's thought that he firmly plants in our minds in the first paragraph of his first chapter: 'But turn off these concrete highways down a side lane or an old main road now by-passed; as in the vortex of a hurricane, you can find complete calm.'

The Kent & East Sussex Railway still steams gently from Tenterden to Bodiam, at Faversham boats still navigate the 'sluggish creek' and moonlight still shines on the dew pond next to the Chanctonbury Ring. Of course if you find yourself out on the Romney Marsh, two miles south of Appledore, you will also see that no one has picked-up the child's toy.

PETER ASHLEY
Slawston 2018

CONTENTS

2   Baroque Monument, Cuckfield Church, Sussex

3   Ash, Kent : the Church and Ship Inn

I

THE VANISHED FOREST

I

IN 1749 Horace Walpole wrote to Montagu, " If you love good roads, conveniences, good inns . . . be so kind as never to go into Sussex . . . Sussex is a great damper of curiosity." In 1935 Hilaire Belloc complained : " But no man can answer for what evil modern machinery may not do in the near future. It may even kill the integrity of the downs." Two points of view. There is a third. With cheap motor transport, trippers on a great scale became inevitable, and mechanised trippers meant concrete roads, petrol pumps, dainty teas and mushroom growths. But—as always in this well-balanced world—an unexpected compensatory factor has now appeared : thirty years ago wheeled traffic used alike the high roads and by-roads ; excursionists and school treats boiled their tea among ruins no matter how inaccessible ; new cottages were built in this small village or that. To-day the motorist, whether in a " Family Ten," a motor coach, or a Rolls, cannot be persuaded to leave his fine concrete road ; surprisingly, bicyclists risk death to accompany him ; yet more surprising, a large number of people doomed to dwell in Tudoresque villas prefer the stink of petrol fumes to the brackish thyme-scent of the downs. In fact, mechanised trippers and mechanised houses are becoming like our main roads—arterialised. But turn off these concrete highways down a side lane or an old main road now by-passed ; as in the vortex of a hurricane, you can find complete calm.

There are exceptions. In spite of the displeasure of bathing in the English Channel and North Sea, bungalows have ousted agriculture from the coasts of Sussex and Kent; and there is the retired business man who has a true love of the country, but no objection to living in an eyesore. (Here he is logical; for his own home cannot interfere with his own view. I have always held that, should one live in an eighteenth-century square with one Edwardian horror—then one should live in the horror.) Finally, there is the hiker, and here we have an analogy : we hikers (I include myself) are on a walking tour; it is only all other walking tourists who deserve the vile name of hiker.

When writing a book of this description the author's first difficulty is to decide where to start, but in this case my decision was simple. I was forced to start from a village in the very centre of these three counties—Surrey, Sussex and Kent. For that is where I live. Twelve years ago I happened to turn down a steep lane of great troughs of Sussex clay. In a wooded valley lay a mill pool—silver among silver reeds, and bulrushes just bursting in white cotton cascades. Mallard and wild duck rose vertically from the marsh; a heron flopped from the great oak to perch ridiculously on top of the purple wood. The mill house was empty, and almost lost among unpruned apple trees, and gooseberry bushes run wild; a simple tile-hung cottage that for four hundred years had refused to fall down.

Above a bridge and a weir, the tranquil mill stream lay among the bulrushes in fat coils, growing narrower and narrower until lost in a thistle-grown marsh. Below the weir it took an amber leap into a frothy pool, then bored across the fields, cutting so deep into the clay that only a line of alders marked its course—in their branches hung debris from last winter's floods. The slopes of the valley were wooded with chestnut and some huge oaks.

Beyond the weir I found a mill wheel so entwined with brambles and bindweed that it could surely never turn again. Rusty Victorian wheel—but an innovation in this valley, replacing the huge hammer that had beaten out the first English-made swords. For this placid pool had been a noisy " hammer pond " ; the silent marsh, the centre of industrial England where forges clapped and boomed and bellows creaked ; while axes chopped in the forest and great oaks toppled on to cracking boughs.

The history of this valley—though no battle was fought—is the history of the Weald. From the pit behind my garage the iron ore was dug. At the farm over the hill—still known as " Huggett's furnace "—the first English cannon was forged.

4   The Author's Home : Tickerage Mill, near Uckfield, Sussex

5   A Dew Pond on the Sussex Downs : Chanctonbury

6   A Hammer Pond on the Sussex Weald : Tickerage

In Elizabeth's reign war-profiteering reached a peak and the profits were sunk in " Armada houses." During brief moments of peace—when there was a home demand only for iron tomb-stones, fire-backs and courtiers' swords — gun-running to pirates made good the deficit. Our fishermen no longer dared leave Rye Harbour, and the Government had to intervene.

By the middle of the eighteenth century, the wealden " black country " was so well established that the discovery of coal made little difference ; the new fuel was shipped from the mines to Sussex ports. But at the end of the century, when the harbours had become silted and the forests had almost disappeared, emigration to the Midlands began ; in 1820 only one hammer was left echoing in the valleys of the weald at Ashburnham—to our great-grandfathers a surviving curiosity, as hand-looms and hand printing-presses are to us to-day.

II

Previous to this industrialisation of Sussex, my stream dribbled undiscovered in a forest that lay unbroken between the north and south ridges of the downs, and spread from Hampshire eastward to the sea. Travel between mediæval villages was on foot or horseback—the shingled church spire a sole guide above the trees. Before that, the forest was traversed only by tracks connecting Saxon settlements at the foot of the downs (the -ings : Poynings, Beeding, Steyning, etc.) with their small forest clearings where swine-herds lived in huts (the -lys, -dens, -hursts and -folds : Hellingly, Tenterden, Hawkhurst, Chiddingfold, etc.). So isolated were these men that they remained for twenty years in ignorance of the Norman Conquest, and were indignant when strange men appeared to assess their land for some foreign king.

Before the coming of the Saxons, who were skilled wood-men, the whole forest lay virgin but for some ribbon develop-ment bordering the Roman roads. The 15th Legion was stationed a few miles south of my valley, and created an oasis of civilisation that in many parts of Sussex has not since been surpassed. It lasted four hundred years, to be quite forgotten— in history, a mere flash as brilliant and momentary as a falling star. The Roman nose survives in Sussex to this day ; and the Roman names, Avis, Virgo, Morphew ; and I know an old hedger with a stage Sussex yokel's fringe of beard whose surname is Venus.

Before this, with forests impenetrable and the seashore a marsh, mankind was left only one choice of habitation : the hilltops, where he could find a few treeless acres for his plough and herds ; for in those days of primitive axes, trees were enough to drive people from the land. On these hilltops we can trace our ancestry back to near-apes. Iron Age, Bronze Age, and the Neolithic Stone Age—their history lies in the chalk of the downs and goes back anything up to 10,000 years ; but in earlier times still, before even the dawn of civilisation, when man lived by hunting, these gameless ridges meant starvation. The few remaining traces of the Mesolithic and Palæolithic existence are to be found on those dry sandy heights that once rose above the sodden forests of the weald.[1]

On the downs, archæologists still trace the outline of fields ploughed by the Romans and Celts, and the footpaths that linked the string of wheat-growing villages ; they still crawl along the galleries of the Cissbury flint mines, which were tunnelled when a pick was an antler and a shovel the shoulder-blade of an ox ; and at Trundle and White-hawk camps they have discovered something of the squalor in which Britons lived more than four thousand years ago. It must have been a very similar life to that of the most primitive African tribes before the white man made them his burden : a semi-nomadic existence, sheltering in ditches and pits. These ancestors of ours cut beads from the chalk, brewed their own mead, and in hard times resorted to cannibalism. They worshipped the Phallus. That was the beginning of our civilisation.

Of pre-civilised Sussex much less is known, but—one of the first of the human species—a gibbering creature—chose to live on the sandy soil of my local golf course at Piltdown, not far from the fifth tee. When he lived can only be conjectured —it may have been several hundred thousand years ago, when Sussex was joined to Africa. Food was plentiful— but dangerous : immense elephants, rhinoceroses and bears. Mentally, this man was developed a shade more, perhaps, than the chimpanzees who drink tea in the Zoo. His bones were

[1] There are, of course, numerous exceptions to this general statement ; a changing climate would at the same time change the character of the land-scape. At one period trees grew on the top of the downs and man was driven to the southern slopes ; at another the drying up of the downland springs forced him into the plains.

unearthed by Sussex labourers in 1912. From an account of
this discovery, we can estimate to what degree the Sussex
intellect had developed during these countless thousands of
years. The archæologist, Charles Dawson, happened to pass
two men digging a gravel pit, and noticed a fragment of an
exceptionally thick skull. He begged the labourers to put aside
anything similar, and to dig with the greatest care. These
labourers " found the greater part, if not the whole of the
human skull . . . and taking it for a cocoanut, deliberately
smashed it . . ." (E. Cecil Curwin, *County Archæologies:
Sussex*).

This Piltdown creature is the first appearance in history of a
Sussex *homo sapiens*—how he came into existence is as mysterious as the arrival of the first wild trout in my stream—but the
geological history of the land can be traced farther back by
milliards of years : the slow process of nature that set the scene
of his birth.

As in Genesis, first there was water ; South-eastern England
was a muddy lake, a few feet deep, peopled by huge reptiles.
The climate was tropical. The sea broke in, and during eons
deposited layer after layer of sand and clay. The great reptiles
disappeared, but in the sea lived microscopic crustaceæ, whose
calcium shells, falling on to the bed of the ocean, produced
in time a layer of chalk. The best indication of the time
factor in the story is that this layer finally reached a
thickness of a thousand feet. Now the sea began to
recede again ; Surrey, Sussex and Kent appeared out of the
water—a great hump of chalk with a core of sand and clay.
Its peak, which was some ten miles south of my valley,
reached three thousand feet.

To-day there is a peculiarity about the rivers of this part of
England : instead of rising in the highest hills, they have their
sources in comparatively low country and cut their way
through the downs. This phenomenon was caused by the
denudation of the weald. Originally, these rivers *did* rise from
the higher points of the chalk hump, and formed great fissures
in its side as they flowed down the northern and southern
slopes. As time went on, they began to wash away the
chalk of the hump until the peak was denuded down to a
ridge of sand standing in a plain. Only the lower slopes
were left as two high ridges of chalk, on one side abrupt
escarpments, on the other falling away gradually to the shore or
cliffs formed by inroads of the sea. One might compare these
parallel ridges to a series of waves : the crests are the North
and South Downs and the high Weald ; the troughs, the north

and south coastal plains and the flat pasture-land of clay. The
Downs and Weald of Sussex, Kent and Surrey; that is the
country we will now explore.

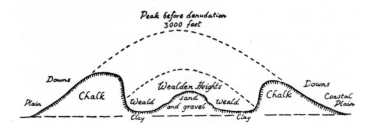

7   Twentieth-century Litter on the Site of a Neolithic Downland Village :
Whitehawk Camp, near Brighton

8 Sussex Chalk : Clayton Down

9 Sussex Clay : the Weald near Buxted

II

NORTH OF THE DOWNS TO TENTERDEN

I

AT the top of my lane we turn left to Cross-in-Hand. Though one of the most beautiful of Sussex place-names, the village has nothing to show for it but a modern inn, a modern church, a windmill that works, and one of the most extensive views in Sussex, taking in forty churches, the Wealds of Sussex and Kent, Ashdown Forest, the coastline of Beachy Head, and the greater part of the Sussex Downs. This is the place to bring a telescope and an argumentative friend—a pleasant morning can be spent that way. But the view is much the same, and just as dull, as any other long-distance view; it is the view from an air liner. Perhaps the aeroplane will prove to a new generation that there can be nothing more dreary than Nature's panoramas.

I know little about windmills, but this windmill at Cross-in-Hand seems to be the latest thing, with its small auxiliary sails which drive themselves round on a circular rail, thus keeping the main sails into wind. I have a grievance against this mill—a grievance which I cannot expect the reader to share. I dislike the fact that it works—it irritates me on my walks to keep catching sight of the revolving silhouette of the sails. For we have a windmill in my own village of Blackboys, a prettier mill though not so up-to-date. During ten years the old miller used to grind my wholemeal flour—I'd watch him at work while everything shuddered and creaked. During a storm the sails were carried away over two fields, and since then the mill at Blackboys has been still, and for sale.

7

Perhaps someone will buy it as a romantic place to live in—
there were rumours of an actress—why, I cannot imagine,
for it is now just a dirty white pepper-pot, with no point
at all.

I have another grievance to do with this part of the world—
but this grievance I hope the reader will share : it is over that
appalling street of Victorian hot brick and cold slate which,
even in spite of the Ordnance map, insists on calling itself
Heathfield.   How could this have been the site of " Hefful
Fair " where for centuries an old woman freed the first cuckoo
of summer from a cage ?   Or the home of that observant
seventeenth-century parson who noted down Halley's comet
in his church register : " A blazing star appeared in this
kingdom.   It did stream from the south west and the middle of
heaven, broader than a rainbow by far " ?

Yet the Post Office, and two A.A. signs, insist that this
outcrop of a railway built on the cheap by an American
contractor is the village of Heathfield.   Drive on (only too
willingly) for a mile or so along the Hastings road, and you
will be puzzled by a sign-post still directing you to " Heathfield
1 Mile."   It is worth while turning down this lane to find one
of the prettiest and smallest of Sussex villages : two rows of
cottages—weather-boarded on one side of the street, and on the
other grey-aged bricks ; a church with a thirteenth-century
tower and shingled spire ; and an inn where—though it is
admitted that to-day there is no old woman to free the cuckoo
at Hefful Fair—they still insist that this first note of summer is
heard on 14th April and on no other date.

In the church a couplet in memory of Thomas Courthope
and his wife proclaims that

> " A happier couple ſure than ne'er was wed
> But much more ſo
> Now they are dead."

II

We rejoin the Eastbourne road at Cade Street, a village
through which traffic speeds.   During the last twelve years
I had passed through this village without knowing its name
until one hot Saturday afternoon.   The road was up, with one-
way traffic ; for many minutes I sat in the August dust waiting
for " Stop " to turn to " Go."   Pneumatic drills were in full
orchestra ; now and again an impatient driver gave an ear-
startling hoot.   Aimlessly my eyes wandered to a square stone

10 Tickerage Wood

11 Tickerage Barn

Around the Author's Home, near Uckfield, Sussex

12   Fun Fair at Uckfield, Sussex

13   The Windmill at Cross-in-Hand, Sussex

monument on the side of the road. I read—for nothing better
to do—the following inscription :

> " Near this spot was slain the notorious rebel
> JACK CADE
> by Alexander Iden esq. Sherif of Kent, A.D. 1460
>
> ---
>
> His body was carried to London, his head fixed on
> London Bridge.
> This is the sweet of all rebels and the fortune chanceth
> ever to traitors."

Cade was an enlightened revolutionary and brilliant general.
As leader of " The Men of Kent " he defeated the King's
forces in one lightning battle and captured London. Having
gained the reforms he demanded, and pardons for all, he dis-
banded his army. Cade himself was tricked ; a name error was
discovered in his pardon, he was hunted down, and shot while
playing a game of bowls.

How changed the scene : I tried to imagine the simple
garden, the bees, the silent arrow. How peaceful this rebel's
death compared with this gibbering afternoon ! [1]

A mile to the south lived another rebel, in the hamlet of
Warbleton. It is a pretty village built on a steep lane ; on one
side slopes a row of three or four cottages and the " War-Bill-
in-Tun " Inn. Opposite stands the church, and, by the churchyard wall, a small farm on the site of the home of Richard
Woodman—worthy, well-to-do iron-master and employer of
many men. In 1557 he rebelled against his Queen, " Bloody
Mary," and led nine other martyrs to the stake.

So little has this hamlet changed that it is not difficult to
imagine this man and his surroundings, and all that took place.
One can see Richard Woodman with his trim pointed beard
and clothes of the best-lasting material bought in Lewes. In
the little inn this rich employer would be listened to with
respect ; his word would be accepted and—should trouble of
any sort arise—these peasants would turn to Mr. Woodman :
he'd soon put things right. We find the same type to-day in
most villages the size of Warbleton : the well-to-do, righteous
local deity. Things did go wrong—very wrong—with the
arrival of the new rector, the Rev. Mr. Fairbanks. Nowadays
such trouble makes third-page news—parishioners send anony-
mous letters, or hide the key of the vestry door. In Warbleton

---

[1] In order to bring the action on to the stage, Shakespeare has Cade struck
down with a sword ; to give pathos he shows the rebel as starving : " Tell
Kent from me she hath lost her best man, and exhort all the world to be cowards ;
for I that never feared any, am vanquished by famine and not by valour "
(*Henry VI.*).

it was left to Woodman to put matters right, and it is easy to imagine the scene in the inn : the lifted tankards, the boasting, " Leave it to Mr. Woodman, he's got the forehorse by the head, he'll tell parson what's right. And we'll stand by him."

Woodman got up in church and told the Rev. Mr. Fairbanks that he was " turning head to tayle," and the little hamlet of Warbleton became more than news, it became history.

The proceedings lasted nearly a year ; the iron-master proved a fine orator. How well one can understand the stubborn loyalty of those nine men and women who put their faith in him, certain that he'd get things put right—Mr. Woodman was a fine one " to arge." But Woodman, did he only wish that he could take back those few words ? We have his own description of his panic flight : " *But yet I got out and leaped down having no shoes, so I took a lane that was full of sharp cinders and they came running after me with a great cry, with their swords drawn crying ' strike him, strike him,' which words made me look back, and there was never one nigh me by a hundred feet ; and all the rest were a greater way behind, and I turned about hastily to go my way and stepped upon a sharp cinder with one foot, and saving of it, I stepped into a great miry hole, and fell down withal, and before I could arise and get away, he was come up to me. His name is Parker the Wild as he is counted in all Sussex.*"

It is the last scene—outside the Star Inn in Lewes—that our imagination cannot visualise in full. Perhaps it is as well. The preparations overnight ; the bouquets of heads at every window ; the soldiers joining pikes to keep back the pressing crowd ; the bickering and jostling and country bumpkin jokes ; the hush of curiosity as the martyrs arrive. The long delay—men cursing and fiddling with knots ; at last the torches, one each side ; the first faint crackle and wisp of blue smoke.

The main interest in the church of Warbleton is the complicated door—designed and worked by this Sussex martyr—said to have been the door of his strong-room. The more morbid liked to think that it was used as his own prison door when he was interned in the church tower.

It is worth while rolling up the carpet in the chancel to see the fifteenth-century brass of Dean William Prestwick. In the canopy above his head the " Pelican of Piety " is seen feeding its young with its own blood. From this legend the Pelican became a symbol of Christ, whose blood, shed on the Cross, is the sacramental sustenance of Christians. In the original Latin version of the hymn by St. Thomas Aquinas, " Thee we

adore, O hidden Saviour, Thee," Christ is directly addressed
as the pelican : " O pie pelicane Jesu " ; but translators un-
courageously gave this as " Fountain of pity, Jesu."

III

Soon after rejoining the Hastings Road the skyline is broken
by an obelisk and two spires. The spire on the right belongs
to the church of Dallington. The other spire will surprise you
as you pass it, for there is no church to be seen, but only the
stucco top of a steeple standing in a field a few yards from the
road. It was put there some hundred years ago by John Fuller
of Rose Hill, one of those odd characters that mark the
eighteenth and early nineteenth centuries : the " Folly "
builders. Fuller is responsible for five : the obelisk on
Brightling Down, this spire top, two observatories, and his
own tomb.

Compared to the great Sussex families, the Fuller family,
in the sixteenth century, was " Nouveau Riche." Their
money came from their forests which supplied the iron
foundries with charcoal. With an honest lack of snobbism the
family took for its motto, " Carbone et Forcipibus."

Jack Fuller was a man of great size (in the House of
Commons he was known as " The Hippopotamus ") and
reputed to have been a proud bully ; but, from his actions,
he appears to have been an intelligent and generous eccentric.
He was a scientist and had a passion for music and painting : he
commissioned Turner to paint a series of landscapes of the
" Rape of Hastings " ; he gave large sums to the Royal
Institution ; he bought Bodiam Castle to save it from ruin ;
to the choir of the church at Brightling he presented nine
bassoons ; on the walls he erected monuments to his friends
whom he admired ; and during the great famine he employed
hundreds of men from all over the country to build his park
wall. Offered a peerage by Pitt, he threw the letter in the fire,
remarking, " Jack Fuller I was born, and Jack Fuller I will
die."

But it is for his " Follies " that this eccentric squire will be
remembered in local history. The obelisk on Brightling Down
is common enough ; the two observatories indulged his
scientific mind ; but the spire top, known locally as the " Sugar
Loaf," must have puzzled many a traveller to the sea. Its origin
could hardly be guessed. One night Fuller boasted to a friend
that he could see Dallington spire from his dining-room

window. Finding next day that he was mistaken, he ordered this top of a spire to be hurriedly built on the skyline, so that it appeared just above the trees.

His last Folly, his tomb, is in the churchyard of Brightling, a colossal stone pyramid that dwarfs all other graves. And in it, Honest John (as he liked to call himself) is said to sit.

It is curious that to-day—only a hundred years later—it is impossible to get this statement either affirmed or denied; still more curious that no effort is made to find out. How many years does good taste decree before a tomb can be opened in the interest of history ? Should this ever happen, I should like to be present ; a flashlight camera would be necessary to make a record before things disintegrated in the air to dust. If Jack Fuller is indeed under this pyramid, the photograph would be unique : a corpse in full evening dress seated before a roast chicken and a bottle of claret.

And the claret ? Ullaged, I fear.

IV

Four miles on, lying in the valley of the Rother, is the small town of Robertsbridge : a long street of fine houses with many bridges, and a trap for the sightseer in a Cistercian Abbey founded in 1176. An S.P.C.S. should be formed—a Society for the Protection of Conscientious Sightseers. Its first duty would be to remove uninteresting ruins that are off the beaten track. The site of Robertsbridge Abbey lies a mile to the east on a pot-holed farm lane. The ruin consists of some rubble with " fragments of arches " now embodied in the walls of a derelict barn. Only to the " sic transit gloria mundi " school of sightseers might Abbey Farm afford a quiet hour of romantic thought ; beneath the rubble rests Sir Thomas Pelham, founder of the famous family whose emblem, a buckle, is seen on so many church walls throughout Sussex. With Sir Roger De la Warr, he captured John, King of France, at the battle of Poitiers. The king surrendered his sword, and the Pelham family took the buckle as their badge ; the De la Warrs the " crampette " or point of the scabbard.

Across the Rother rises the fourteenth-century spire of Salehurst Church, which is also the church of Robertsbridge. Why it should stand in this hamlet instead of the town is surprising, and was more so centuries ago, when an arm of the sea intervened, and the devout of Robertsbridge had to be ferried to church.

14 Bodiam Castle, East Sussex

15   Approaching Tenterden

16   The Junction at Robertsbridge
The Kent and East Sussex Railway

From the back of the church a " precipice " of a road leads
up over Silver Hill to Bodiam. " Without being at all killed,"
Walpole wrote in 1750, " we got up or down—I forget which,
it was so dark—a famous precipice called Silver Hill and about
ten arrived at a wretched village called Rotherbridge." How
well one understands that irritation common to all tourists
after an overlong day, when every hotel is dirty, and every
church is bad. My four-year-old car climbed Silver Hill
without effort on top.

V

If you have the time and curiosity, continue your journey
from Robertsbridge to Tenterden by rail. Time is needed
when there is much shunting to be done, for it may then take
you an hour and a quarter to cover the fifteen miles ; curiosity,
because the " Kent and East Sussex " is one of the last remaining privately owned Railway Companies in England. The
little black dirty engine was once the pride of the L.B. & S.C.
Railway. Then it had wooden brakes and was painted
gamboge. In the interim it saw war service in France. The
guard is at the same time porter, shunter, ticket-salesman,
ticket - collector, and pointsman as well. At the only two
level-crossings which are protected from motor traffic, the
fireman gets down to open and shut the gates ; at the
others, the war veteran slows down from twenty-five to two
miles an hour, and the whistle lets out an old man's throaty
croak.

Unlike the Roman roads which preferred the hilltops, this
track clings to the river Rother, which is here the boundary
between Sussex and Kent. There is only one perceptible slope
—beyond Rolvenden—and the engine's puffed complaints
reminded me of one of my grandfather's railway jokes :
" Ithinkican. . . . I think I can. . . . I—think—I—can. . . .
I —— think —— I —— can. . . . I —— think ——.
. . . I —— thought —— I —— could. . . . I — thought —
I—could. . . . I thought I could. . . . Ithoughticould . . .
Ithoughticouldithoughticouldithoughticould."

The track, as green and beautiful as a chickweedy disused
canal, finds its way through hedges of willows which rap and
brush the carriage sides, or across Bodiam marshes where
herons stand by the line—no longer perturbed. There are few
roads through this stretch of country, which remains much the
same as when the peasants first complained about the iron

monster which had desecrated their land. The view from the carriage windows is that private view common to most railways, but in this case exclusive : I had never seen Bodiam Castle from this angle before.

Bodiam was my one disappointment; like the Taj Mahal this castle is best seen in its most hackneyed view. When I take my guests sight-seeing, I persuade them to walk blindfolded across the meadows to be astonished by the dramatic grey fortress precisely reflected in the wide moat. This moat, together with barbican, drawbridge and portcullis, and four staunch round towers gives an impression of impregnable strength. But we can search history in vain to find any record of the castle having fired or received a single round shot. There was, originally, a private mansion here which Sir Edward Dalyngrudge " crenellated " in 1386, but the crenellations remained ornaments until the Civil War, when the castle was ignobly dismantled by Waller's troops. Much the same applies to Hurstmonceux, ten miles to the south. Here again we find a flooded moat and every mediæval machination of defence. But these superb walls of lichened brick represent the domestic architecture of the late fifteenth century. It was almost the first building of size to be built of brick since Roman times, but is little more related to warfare than a Puginesque Gothic railway station to a House of God. Bodiam Castle, after passing through many hands—first as a mansion, then a ruin—was finally purchased by the late Lord Curzon and presented to the National Trust. Hurstmonceux, after being partially dismantled in the eighteenth century by the architect Wyatt, was restored to some extent by the late Sir Claude Lowther. But it was left to the present owner, Sir Paul Lathom, to devote several years' care, ingenuity and income to recreating a spectacular and magnificent private house.

Northiam appeared to be an important station : I was joined by a passenger with a perambulator ; and some endless shunting was done. The guard-pointsman could give no fixed time of departure, but he would hold the train for me, of course, if I wished to walk up the village for a glass of beer. The village is a complete example of weather-boarded architecture—the cottages, decorated with black window-frames and broad black bands on white, presenting an entertaining magpie effect. Near the church are propped the remains of a senile oak ; it will never be allowed to fall down, for Queen Elizabeth picnicked under its shade when on her way from Hemstead to Rye. The fare was cooked in the timbered house which still stands across the road ; and a heavy meal it must have been, accompanied by some fine bottles of wine, for the Queen had to remove her high-heeled shoes (oh, blessed relief !)—and quite forgot to put them on again. They are still preserved at Northiam, in the half-timbered manor, Brickwall : green silk shoes with heels nearly three inches high. Brickwall, once the seat of the Frewen family, is now a school. Its zebra-striped front can be seen from the road—absolutely genuine and absolutely hideous.

The little train pulled into Tenterden with pride and relief ; I walked up a lane behind the church into a grass-bordered street so wide that it is almost a village green. When I looked back at the old-fashioned station with its ornamental gas lanterns, it seemed already older than the houses in the town. In fact, there are not more than half a dozen buildings in this most agreeable street later than the eighteenth century, and only one that has actually been seduced by the functional cinema palace. It belongs to the Wealden Electricity Company and, standing next door to the cinema, its temptation was, I suppose, too strong. The seduction has given birth to a freak : the modern shop front reaches half-way up the original eighteenth-century façade, but juts thirty feet out on to the street—in its centre stands the old white porticoed doorway flanked by two sheets of plate glass.

The church tower is an impressive landmark from far out across the Romney marshes, but Sandwich shipping merchants of the sixteenth century used to regard it with distaste. The harbour had begun to silt up, and this tower was blamed; its stones — they claimed — had been quarried from the breakwater that had held back the shifting Goodwin Sands. So strong was their resentment that Sir Thomas Moore was sent to hold an enquiry. The chief witness was the oldest inhabitant.

" . . . I am well nigh an hundreth years old," he offered as evidence, " . . . and I may remember the building of Tenter-ton steeple, and I may remember when there was no steeple at all there. And before that Tenterton steeple was in building, there was no manner of speaking of any flats or sands that stopped the haven, and therefor I think that Tenterton steeple is the cause of the destroying and decaying of Sandwich haven."

Fortunately, reasoning so empirical was not thought sufficient evidence that Tenterden's graceful tower should be returned to the sea.

VI

Though the hotel is simple, this village makes a pleasant centre for exploring all the other " -*dens* "; and the " -*hursts* " as well. The -*hursts* lie scattered along the Kent Ditch : Hawkhurst, Sandhurst, Ewhurst, Ticehurst, Wadhurst, Lamberhurst, Goudhurst, Sissinghurst—I have lost countless bets as to which are in Sussex and which in Kent. But they have one thing in common : their weather-boarded houses—a tradition that has never died out. Æsthetically this seems a taste-proof medium ; weather-boarded houses cannot be ugly—but cannot reach the grandeur of stone or brick.

I had time only to visit a few of these first Saxon settlements (the " dens " were dells, the " hursts " woods) : Hawkhurst I made a note of because, within its fringe of modern brick, are hidden some of the best wooden buildings in Kent ; one in particular, a small eighteenth-century house with black window-frames and fanlight, is as pretty as can be. If you should become nauseated with prettiness, there is a cure close at hand in Highgate : an original parish church designed by Sir Gilbert Scott. It has all the horror of a late Victorian billiard room— and exactly the same smell. If your cure is incomplete, stop at Kilndown Church, on your way to Goudhurst. Built in 1840, the interior is painted from ceiling to floor—pulpit, chancel screen, reredos and font—in pillar-box red, Reckitt's blue, and gilt, and all lit by windows of Munich glass. Here is a building that Scott would have been justified in pulling down ; or should we perhaps be grateful it escaped ? Such painstaking ugliness has created a collector's piece.

In Ticehurst Church there is some fourteenth-century stained glass which gives a lurid picture of the Catholic superstition of the time that flames, boiling cauldrons and other such horrors awaited the ungodly in after life. The drawing is naïf —a cartload of sinners is depicted being drawn into Hell by a little devil who has all the charm of Mickey Mouse. The colour is excellent, and so, no doubt, was the design. But, like much of England's stained glass, this has been reassembled from fragments left by Cromwell, and these windows have the inevitable jigsaw-puzzle effect.

Goudhurst climbs steeply to the Perpendicular church which stands facing an inn almost as ancient. The church is best known for the forty Culpeper monuments and brasses ; but they are dull compared to the Renaissance tomb of William

17 Tenterden, Kent: the architectural patchwork of the main street

18   Timber and Shingles : the Church at High Halden, Kent

Campion, who was killed in 1642 defending the cause of Charles I. at the Siege of Colchester.

Lamberhurst Church is hard to find—for it stands in mid-country half a mile away from the village—but is well worth visiting for its seventeenth-century pulpit, which is the most beautiful in Kent.

Sissinghurst possesses a castle whose astonishing central tower dominates the landscape as a " Folly "—but a folly of beauty. This tower, a gateway, and some outer buildings are all that remain of a huge mansion built in the seventeenth century by Sir John Baker, who—on account of his sadistic persecution of Protestants—was known to his contemporaries as " Bloody Baker." In the beginning of the eighteenth century the property went out of the hands of the Baker family, and during the next two hundred years suffered many changes of ownership ; suffered by being put to every possible humilia-tion. It was alternately used as a prison for French soldiers during the Seven Years War, labourers' cottages, and a house for the poor.

The house has now come back to a direct descendant of Bloody Baker, the poetess Vita Sackville-West, who with her husband, Harold Nicolson, has devoted the last ten years to creating a garden out of a rubbish-heap. " Not only were the immediate surroundings a mere wilderness of weeds," she writes, " but most of the original buildings had either fallen down or been pulled down to provide material for building elsewhere. The entrance porch was bricked up ; the windows mere holes with banging, broken shutters ; the roofs threatened to cave in ; the walls had either in part collapsed or were so overgrown with brambles and other rubbish as to render it impossible to guess that any wall was there until the work of clearance began."

This summer I was shown green courtyards, on which wheeling white pigeons cast fluttering shadows, flower-beds that paid homage to June, and a house that had been more than restored—it had been saved.

VI

The -dens, unlike the -hursts, belong almost exclusively to Kent. Bethersden, Biddenden, Devils den, Rolvenden, Eagles den, Silver den, Benenden, Pips den and Dingle den, they lie in a string a few miles east of the " Ditch."

Architecturally, Tenterden is unsurpassed ; but Biddenden

draws the crowd. The village has crazy paving, leaning half-timbered cottages, a row of black-and-white almshouses, and, above all, an attractive legend on which it thrives. Here lived England's first recorded " Siamese " twins : the " Biddenden maids." So devoted were they that when one died the other refused to be severed from her sister—an operation that would have saved her life. With that curious vanity of freaks, they perpetuated their memory by leaving a plot of land to the village—the rent to be spent on an annual gift of cakes to the villagers ; twin cakes in their likeness— joined together as they were—and stamped with their names.

For smug rural charm visit Benenden—it is best seen during a cricket match on a hot Saturday afternoon ; to· each small tile-hung cottage there must be an acre of village green. It is so easy to visualise a similar match played a hundred years ago: only the top-hats are missing, and the Dundreary whiskers ; and perhaps the scorer should have a bottle of claret beneath his chair. Otherwise, everything is just as sleepily, deliciously respectable : standing on a prominence, the church still dominates the playing-field in spite of its size ; there is a Georgian weather-boarded Post Office with a charming colonnade, an inoffensive war memorial hall erected by the land-owning peer, and a village schoolhouse so anxious not to be conspicuous that it has managed, somehow, to fit in. On a summer evening, when the horse-chestnuts were in bloom, this sweet playground of a Kentish village seemed to deny all possibility of horrid dictators making war. Or could it, I wondered, be the cause ?

III

ACROSS THE WEALD INTO KENT

I

BEFORE the denudation of the Weald, the ridge upon which Mayfield stands was the highest point in South-eastern England. It is still the most important watershed, feeding the Rother, the Ouse and the Medway. The village has a fine street of old houses, a dull church, a spectacular half-timbered hotel and a Bishop's palace.

The palace was once a building on a pretentious scale; according to Birchington, " Archbishop Islip wasted more of the timber in the Dourden than any of his predecessors." It proved a waste indeed; for this palace was fated to become a complete ruin and be restored by Pugin. Now a convent, it is open to the public only four hours a week; during twelve years in the neighbourhood I have not yet timed my visit correctly.

There are three legends connected with Mayfield: one concerns the half-timbered hotel, once a private house known as " The Middle House." It is a museum piece and should be visited for the carved panelling in the dining-room and the overmantel in the main hall, said erroneously to be by Grinling Gibbons. For the legend you must climb beneath the rafters in the roof. Here, somewhere at the beginning of the seventeenth century, a former owner kept his wife locked up for ten years while he lived with his mistress downstairs. I found the cramping attic just as it was three hundred years ago. I saw the door with wooden bars through which the woman was fed, and the original lock and chain. A new bath lay outside the door and coils of lead piping. Next day the plumbers were due to start work.

The other two legends concern St. Dunstan. The first

church at Mayfield—then called Magavelda—was of wood.
When completed it was found not to be oriented true East
and West. The Saint leant against the wall and *aliquantulum
presit* the church into its proper position. This miracle is
probably founded on truth; it is not difficult to imagine
the little building no bigger than a hencoop; the foreman
scratching his forehead: "Bless me—if we haven't got her
out of true"; St. Dunstan's hearty "Come on then, lads,
all together—one, two, three, heave!"

The other miracle—with its rapid change of scene—is as
inconsequential as a dream, and the Saint's behaviour would
not be thought "cricket" under the present-day English
moral code. The story starts somewhere near Brighton,
when the Devil, who had decided to destroy Sussex, has the
grace to allow St. Dunstan the choice of the manner in which
it should be done. St. Dunstan appears to play into the
Devil's hands, deciding that his people would prefer to be
drowned. Considering the geological formation of Sussex,
he could not have made a more foolish choice; for the Devil
proceeded that night to dig a channel through that high ridge
of chalk which protects the county from the sea. St. Dunstan
now had to resort to a series of tricks only justified against
the enemies of God. First he made a wager with the Devil
and then cheated; he bet him that he could not complete
the work by dawn—if he failed, Sussex would be saved. The
Devil was confident, and within a few hours he had dug a
dyke which is still called by his name, and thrown up those
great mounds of chalk now known as Chanctonbury and
Cissbury Rings. But in the meanwhile St. Dunstan had
visited all the neighbouring farms and persuaded every cock
to crow two hours before dawn. Others say that it was the
farmers' wives he persuaded to light candles in their windows.
Whichever way it was, the Devil was mystified and climbed
the summit of the nearest hill, only to find no sign of day.
He realised that he had been tricked, but an hour or more
had been wasted and the wager was lost.

Now the scene moves unexpectedly some thirty miles to
Mayfield, where the Devil flew in order to remonstrate with
St. Dunstan. The Saint discussed the matter with apparent
patience and reason, while he heated in his furnace a pair of
enamelling tongs. It was not until they were red hot that he
brought out an argument that carried weight: he clapped the
tongs on to his opponent's nose.

In one leap the Devil landed on the hill across the valley,
and there he found a cool spring in which to soothe his pain.

19 The Village Street, Mayfield, Sussex

20   Calverley Crescent, Tunbridge Wells

21   A Terrace in Hove

His nose is said to have given the water mysterious healing powers which bring the sick to this same spring to-day—unlike all other pilgrim shrines, this place, now famous as Tunbridge Wells, is in fact a shrine of Old Nick.

But those who dislike such a thought can be reassured : the chalybeate springs of Tunbridge Wells were discovered accidentally by the over-indulged Lord North when visiting the Earl of Abergavenny in 1606. Thirty years later (by which time he should have been more or less cured) he published a pamphlet pointing out that it was no longer necessary to go to the expense and hardships of a journey to a German spa. At this time there was not even a village at the " Wells " and the first invalids had to find lodging in Tonbridge—hence the double name. As with almost every spa, these waters required a livery peer to start their fashion ; a royal hypochondriac to seal it : Queen Henrietta Maria came here as such, and, after her son's restoration to the throne, the Court, with all its " smarties " and hangers-on, turned the Tonbridge wells into a fashionable pleasure resort.

There was still no proper accommodation—but this seems to have been the main attraction : booths were set up under the trees, and labourers' cottages and shepherds' huts were transported bodily on sledges to form a very rural—but very *chic*—colony of dyspeptics.

" To these huts, men of fashion, wearied with the din and smoke of London, sometimes came in the summer to breathe fresh air and to catch a glimpse of rural life. During the season a kind of fair was daily held near the fountain. The wives and daughters of the Kentish farmers came from the neighbouring villages with cream, cherries, wheatears and quails. To chaffer with them, to flirt with them, to praise their straw hats and tight heels, was a refreshing pastime to voluptuaries sick of the airs of actresses and maids of honour."

Weather permitting, it must have been a most entrancing picnic, and the landscape of heather, beech glades and artificial-looking rocks, the perfect stage setting. And how theatrical the scene must have appeared—as theatrical as the last scene in a musical comedy when every character is made to assemble, irrespective of time or place. For here in the primitive jungle of the Weald, bazaars and shopping booths spread their wares under the trees : trinkets and costly jewellery, the latest astonishing hat, and, for the spoilt bored children, expensive novelties in toys.

The dyspeptic dandies had their coffee rooms and gambling

D

clubs—and even newspapers, though they arrived from London many days old. All night the gaiety of fiddles explored the wild valleys, and there was dancing on the natural sandy turf. It must have been a yet more fanciful scene when the new church (which was dedicated to St. Charles the Martyr) was completed, a magnificent red-brick edifice, built by subscription, and the only solid building standing in the forest beside the well.

The church is inconspicuous to-day among the new buildings of the town, but the interior, with its extravagantly moulded ceiling, still recalls the days when this was one of the most fashionable places of worship in England. Evidence of the town's later prosperity can be seen in the " Pantiles," a graceful pillared promenade that encloses the well, and Calverly Crescent, laid out by Decimus Burton, who designed the screen at Hyde Park Corner. There is little else of architectural merit, but there is an object in the town that must have excited such universal curiosity that I feel bound to include it in this book. You will see it as you drive towards Tonbridge, on the right of the road among the houses, as if forming part of a terrace—a full-sized steamer with ventilators, davits, signal flags, black-and-red funnel and white mast. I had wondered for many years what this Folly could be ; the writing of this book gave me the courage to inquire. I rang the bell of the nearest house, which proved to be a private school. The headmaster was pleased to show me round—with reason ; for he and his pupils had built with their own hands this strange vessel stranded on dry land. Everything is complete and in working order : wheel, compass, and even a dinghy which can be lowered from the davits on to the lawn. Below deck is a large saloon, and here the schoolmaster's ingenuity shows supreme : the forward wall lets down to disclose a Reredos. This earthbound ship is the school chapel.

II

A few miles to the east of Tunbridge Wells are the ruins of Bayham Abbey. The beauty of mediæval ruins must depend on their setting ; they can no longer be considered as architecture ; æsthetically they are formless and dull. But there are some, such as Bayham, which play their part—striking a romantic note in a romantic landscape.

I came to the ruins one first spring evening—or rather,

an evening that winter had stolen from spring; February was not yet through, and there was no one to take my sixpence admission—no one in sight or hearing. I walked down the gentle slope of meadow and crossed the little river Teise which was still flooded from melting snow. Beyond the wooden bridge, the ruins stood among cedars and marshy ground. The sun set behind a hard ridge of oaks, while rooks came sailing raggedly—a black broken army—across a metallic sky. A mist rose from the slough to hang like astral spirits among the broken arches of the choir.

The nave is long and narrow as a corridor, and without aisles. Congregations were not welcomed by the austere Premonstratensian canons who prayed here seven hundred years ago—processions were forbidden. In spite of this the local peasants regarded the order with esteem. When the canons were expelled in the Reformation the simple villagers painted their faces to frighten the King's commissioners away.

There is another expedition which I can recommend: to Withyham Church with its stupendous altar-tomb to Richard, Earl of Dorset (d. 1677), by Caius Gabriel Cibber. The chapel contains several other De La Warr monuments, and it is instructive to follow the decline in taste through Nollekens, Flaxman and Chantrey down to a pitiable plaque erected in 1915. On the way to Withyham you pass through Groombridge, a show village that has not yet learnt to show off.

III

Continuing our journey eastward we come to Tonbridge, the greater part of which is taken up by Victorian Gothic school-buildings, playing-fields, fives-courts and gym. The pleasantest parts are the Rose and Crown Hotel—now the centre of local life—and the castle grounds. When first built, this castle was of sufficient importance to have been exchanged, after a complicated family dispute, for the Royal Castle of Brion in Normandy. To-day the walls make a superb bed for rock plants, and only the main gateway stands intact among public gardens and lawns.

North-east to Maidstone the main road and by-roads follow the valley of the Medway through " The Garden of England " —so called because most of the land is given up to the making of cider and beer. During early spring every view must be seen through a pattern of blossom or a cat's-cradle of thin poles and knotted flax. It is a curious landscape : gaunt alleys for ever changing their perspective, and—more curious still—the unexpected sight of slow striding figures on stilts. Every farmhouse—almost every cottage—has its group of oast-houses. They have a certain beauty which reaches a climax at Beltring in Whitbread's hop farm with its twenty-four conical towers each capped by a starch-white cowl. This is the beauty of functionalism, and I find it vaguely irritating to see an oast-house that no longer functions except as a tired Londoner's week-end retreat.

There are few roads that can offer such varied sightseeing as this fifteen-mile stretch to Maidstone. No sooner have we left the outskirts of Tonbridge than a " Folly " like the Tower of Babel dwarfs every poplar and spire. It is the tower of Victorian Hadlow Castle built by Squire May. In common with Squire Fuller's pyramid at Brightling, the object of this Folly is disputed in the village bar; but whatever his reason, May appears to have wasted his money. It is said that he wished to have a view of the North Sea; but on completion it was found that the North Downs still intervened. Alternatively his wish was to be buried at the top of the tower in order to defeat a prophecy that his home would go out of the family unless he remained above-ground. Some say a compromise was effected : he now stands above-ground in his tomb (which is the size of a cottage) in the corner of the churchyard. Unavailing—since Squire May's death, Hadlow Castle has changed hands. More malicious is the story that after his wife had left him for a farmer, he was determined that, wherever she might be in Kent, she must see his tower and regret ; but her love proved stronger than any reminder of the Victorian comforts of her old home. It may be, on the other hand, that Squire May, in common with most Folly builders, only wished to purchase some sort of immortality at any cost. If such was the case, I pray that his wish may be granted through this book.

A few miles on we pass two buildings that some would like to include among the " Follies " of Kent. It was the folly of a vandal, they say, when John Fane, the seventh Earl of Westmorland, transformed a thousand acres of " The Garden of Kent " into a landscape garden of un-English beauty. He pulled down the old parish church and rectory to build Palladian Mereworth Castle with its temples and avenues, and a church of his own creation which, admittedly, comes as a shock. Though the old church and rectory must always

22　The Kentish Weald near Ashford

23   Moonlight in Kent

be sentimentally regretted, Westmorland should receive due praise for having employed Colin Campbell to lay out his garden and build his house. Campbell may have been a copyist, who made little effort to blend Italian and English traditions, but few English architects knew, as he did, how to build country houses on a grand scale combining such elegance and charm.

The second Folly, the church, designed by the Earl, cannot be taken as seriously as the house. The Baroque spire supported on a semicircular arcade is a pretty invention, but after that the amateur architect seems to have lost his inspiration; the remainder of his exterior, with its bare walls and slate roof, looks like a railway-siding shed. The interior, on the other hand, is a complete success: the thirty-six imitation marble columns, the painted imitation plasterwork on the ceiling, and the semicircular window filled with a glory of amber glass produce a gay stage effect. Hidden away behind the robing room is a seventeenth-century Westmorland monument removed from the old church: an elaborate Baroque monument with painted canopy and gilded cherubs. It should be brought out of hiding to become the focal point.

Beyond the boundaries of the Park, at Netherfield, stands another small church, one that cannot fail to appeal to all who find it. But to find it during April is not easy, for it stands off the road in an orchard, and the grey stone is as pale as the shadow among the blossom and the half-tones of the showering clouds. I had passed it by a mile or more, but luckily decided to turn back. It is unique, this doll's cathedral, for the Perpendicular windows—large and flamboyant, out of all proportion to the simple fabric—still frame their fifteenth-century glass. In spite of the lateness of the date these windows are inspired by the integral vision of the Byzantine tradition. The canopies and jewels have a richness never achieved in modern stained glass. We must be grateful to those who subscribed towards the restoration of these windows, but it is unfortunate that the restoration should have been carried too far—better a few gaps in the pattern than those bad-tempered Victorian faces so ill fitting their joyous robes.

IV

The conscientious sightseer should spend the rest of his day in Maidstone with its Museum, important Perpendicular

Church, Archbishop's Palace, College of All Saints, and old
houses and bridge. To give him strength I can recommend the
Royal Star Hotel, which has an excellent restaurant, grill room
and snack bar, and—judging from the list—some acceptable
wines. But if the day should happen to be that rare English
gift—a summer's day in April—then remember that Maidstone
is not all mediæval; for the most part it is a noisy, twentieth-
century, tram-ridden, traffic-jammed town. On such a day
cut north to the Mallings and then cross the Medway at
Aylesford by the ancient humpbacked bridge; we now have
left the land of " The Men of Kent " for the land of " Kentish
Men," and are bound for the purest landscape in this corner
of England : the eastern stretch of the Winchester Pilgrims'
Way, and those narrow roads that climb over the North
Downs.

Aylesford is Aegaelsford in the Saxon Chronicle. Perhaps
the name was derived from Eglwys, which would have meant
church-ford, or perhaps it was Eagle's-ford; alternatively,
it is possible that, like Aylesbury, the name was a tribute to
the memory of the great mythical archer from the north—
Egil, who was the origin of William Tell. But it is the second
syllable that has played so important a part in the early history
of this village. In the surrounding hills are monuments
to prehistoric chieftains ; " Kits Coity House " stands im-
pressively alone in a ploughed field, four huge stone slabs,
propped together like the first story of a house of cards.
How has it been allowed to survive all these centuries ? Was
it superstition, or the sheer weight of the stones which kept
them protected until the archæologists surrounded the monument with spiked iron railings ? Nearby are the " Countless
Stones " whose number no man can gauge, and the " Coffin
Stone." All around lie the bones from unrecorded battles
—the Carnac of Kent. Whether it was here that Horsa fell,
and Hengist was crowned king, is disputed, but there is
little doubt that the Saxon army, having crossed over from
the Isle of Thanet and marched along the Roman road—
only to find the bridge at Rochester destroyed—would
have turned south to fight a battle for the possession of
Aegels-ford. It was not until the appearance of the stone-
arched bridge that this village lost its strategic importance, and found peace. And wealth too, it would appear ;
the Culpeper and Banks monuments in the church are
among the most magnificent in Kent. Of the latter-day
homeliness of this village—for centuries the battlefield of
the South-East—we can read in *Pickwick* ; not a mile away

24 Hollingbourne Church

25 Aylesford Church

Kentish Baroque Monuments

26 From the Pilgrims' Way near Sevenoaks, Kent

27 Georgian Farmhouse at Littlebourne, Kent

is the scene of Winkle's disgrace — the skating pond of Dingly Hall.[1]

V

We can pick up one of the Pilgrims' Ways at " Kits Coity House." At its best it is a narrow metalled road, at its worst (but pleasantest) a footpath. For fast motoring I cannot even recommend the best—there is a fine tarmac road that runs parallel a mile or two to the south. Was it through expedience or from sentiment, one wonders, that the County Council chose to develop this lower road and leave the Pilgrims' Way a track ?

It was somewhere above Boxley that I first discarded my prejudice against the North Downs—a prejudice planted by chalk country purists who refuse to admit that these hills with their top dressing of clay and wooded slopes are downs at all. In fact, they are wrong ; this is just as true a picture of prehistoric England as the billiard-ball ridges of Sussex and Wiltshire. At that time our climate was suffering extreme changes—during the wettest cycles, forests spread over the hilltops. J. C. Maby, B.Sc., has identified, from Neolithic and Bronze-Age charcoal, some twenty different trees and shrubs that at one period covered our whole stretch of downs.

On this April evening I looked up at a patterned hillside as beautiful as any I know : the yew groves made an indigo background for soft sprays of cherry blossom, and hawthorn in dabs of virile green ; the elders were still bleached skeletons, the burgeoning oaks their queer drab autumn tint ; at precise intervals the whole pattern was cut knife-edged by little cliffs of chalk. Drive up one of the many lanes that branch north off the Pilgrims' Way ; they cut through forty-foot yew hedges as giant garden paths. Walk over the turfy hilltops and look down on the Weald of Kent ; against each wild downland spur, blossom breaks in foam.

On one of these side roads, among a sprinkling of Tudor cottages, you will find the church of Lynsted. You must make a point of finding it because it shelters one of the most beautiful monuments in Kent : Baron Christopher Roper lies under a classical pediment of coloured marbles—pink, amber, and greyish blue. His armour has been left pale untinted stone except for a touch of gamboge on the sword-

[1] At that time the home of a Farmer Sprong, a friend of Dickens ; now the house of Sir Tyrwhitt Drake. In the grounds is the famous Maidstone Zoo.

hilt and belt. He wears a cloak of faded Indian red. These soft colourings and the repeated horizontal lines seem to insist on death's repose. His wife kneels living beside him— a startling vertical note in black; and her cowled head-dress billows behind her in a metallic arc. On the front of the tomb are two plaques carved by Epiphanius Evesham. His portrayal of the mourning relatives is more than a work of beauty. Look closely at these women in their ruffs and feathered head-dresses, poke bonnets or tilted boaters; some are holding their tear-damp handkerchiefs, another carries her pet dog; you can gauge their grief to a fraction; some are desolate; but the pretty girl in the boater feels no sorrow at all. This is surely a vital portrait of three hundred years ago; you go out into the blossomed village street as if waking from a dream.

It would be unwise to lay down an itinerary for these by-ways of the North Downs, for it is by haphazard exploration that they can be best enjoyed. But do not accelerate through the village of Detling, just because the estate agents proclaim that they are about to build: in the church is a dateless, nameless carving of a man in prayer—an emotional work of art. Nor should you miss the turning to Hollingbourne Church which stands in a lane branching off the main Maidstone road. Here are three unusual monuments and the famous Culpeper altar-cloth worked over three hundred years ago.

Marshall's white marble effigy of Lady Elizabeth Culpeper is unusual because, unlike most seventeenth-century tombs in England, it is neither mutilated nor scratched with a single tourist's name. There is only the broken ear of her dog to show the wear of three centuries.

Lady Elizabeth's four daughters embroidered the altar-cloth. During all the years that Cromwell dictated to England, they worked secretly in a dark underground room. One sister never saw the finished work when it was presented to the church the day that Charles II. returned to the throne— she was blind. The cloth, which is now kept in the rectory, is of funereal purple velvet embroidered with a border of fruit and flowers. Its value lies only in its romantic history and age.

Apart from its very great charm, the Baroque monument to Grace Getting has a special appeal to an author: Grace was an author herself and she is shown kneeling between two angels and displaying with pride her own book—a best-seller of the time. But there is more than that to stir the interest and envy of all writers—and publishers as well; it was not until several years after her death, when this monument had been carved, as well as replicas for Westminster Abbey and Bath, that her book was discovered to have been " lifted " from the first page to the last.

I had almost forgotten my third unusual monument in Hollingbourne Church : a marble plaque to the memory of a boy, Archie Dappa, whose photograph—a daguerrotype of the 'eighties—forms the major part of the design.

We come to a break in the chalk at Chilham ; it was here that the river Stour decided—some hundreds of thousands of years ago—to cut its way through the ridge of down. The village stands just off the main road—or has been by-passed—and is now unnoticed by the traffic stream. It is worth a moment's halt to see this pleasant village-square of half-timbered cottages, and to quarrel over the Baroque monument to Lady Digges which is in the church. Four oversized female figures in white marble are grouped round a lofty black column. The proportions of the monument are perhaps faulty, but these figures seem to me to have a plastic significance—something of the vision of Picasso in their static weight.

Chilham Castle, in its mediæval form, was pulled down by its owner, Sir Thomas Cheyney, whose tomb and character we discuss later in Minster Church. The present house, which is one of many once said to have been designed by Inigo Jones, became front - page news a year or two ago, when it was the home of the late Sir Edmund Davis, million-aire and enthusiastic patron of arts. His collection of old masters was his main joy in life ; one morning three of the most valuable were found cut from their frames. In response to a generous reward, one of the thieves came forward with two paintings—and was arrested by the police. The third masterpiece has never been traced and is believed to have been destroyed out of revenge. The police were, of course, acting strictly according to their duty ; but art lovers may ask whether, on this occasion, they did not overstep the mark.

VI

Too weary to face Canterbury I went on to Fordwich (better known to anglers as Fordidge) to spend the night. I chose a roundabout route which I recommend : along the valley of the " Little Stour," and through Wickhambreaux with its curious Flemish post-office ; and a mill pool reflecting the gold of laburnum trees and the starch-white mill.

Three hundred years ago Izaak Walton wrote : " There is also in Kent, near to Canterbury, a trout called there a Fordidge trout . . . that is accounted the rarest of fish ; many of them near the bigness of a salmon . . . and none of these have been known to be caught with an angle, unless it were one that was caught by Sir George Hastings, an excellent angler, and now with God."

I spent a night at Fordwich because I am one of those patient lunatics who choose to fish for trout with a fly made of feathers, when—as every schoolboy knows—trout much prefer fat wriggling worms. In Walton's time all methods were considered fair : " Trout is usually caught with a worm," he writes, " or a minnow which some call a penk. . . ." But he seems to have come to the conclusion that the Fordwich trout (which we now know to be a sea trout) eat nothing at all ; and he even allows himself a slight note of irritation, unusual in a fisherman : " And so much for these Fordidge Trouts which never afford an angler sport, but either live by the virtue of fresh water only ; or as the birds of Paradise and the cameleon are said to live, by the sun and the air."

What would he have written of the Fordwich fishing to-day ? Would he have complained, I wonder, of the traffic hooting over the bottle-neck bridge ; of the children tiddlering with jam jars—throwing them out with a splosh on the end of a string ; of the sea scouts racing in rowing-boats ; of the queue of rods waiting their turn at Sturry mill pool ? I doubt it. We smiled good evening to each other as we jostled past on the bank—even offered the loan of a special deadly fly. None of us noticed the traffic, nor the jam jars, nor the racing scouts ; our eyes were strained on a feathered alder half lost in the reflected dusk ; our ears tuned only to the suck of a monster rise round the bend. And when we all met later, long after dark, in the bar of the George and Dragon, we were still smiling amiably as we ordered our pints and settled down to discuss the fish that no one had caught.

But I have neglected those who refuse to fish—there *are* other interests in Fordwich : a half-timbered town-hall, for instance, said to be the smallest in England, which exhibits on the first floor (charge 6d.) a ducking-stool, and a drying-

28 The River Stour at Fordwich, Kent

29   Lynsted Church, Kent

30   Stoke D'Abernon Church, Surrey

Elizabethan Monuments

room for ducked wives.   In the church is an unusual sarco-
phagus—" The oldest example of monumental work in Kent "
—thought, by the credulous, to be the tomb of St. Augustine ;
and three windows, each with a double arch and quatrefoil,
that are almost as beautiful a sight as a rising fish.

CHAPTER

IV

PILGRIM CITY

NEXT morning, as I crossed Sturry bridge, I saw a
grey tower dominating the landscape : Canterbury—
England's premier showplace for tourists of the world.
Compared to Salisbury, the Cathedral is a magnificent jumble ;
the ground plan, which hangs in the nave, shows an asym-
metrical maze of Nave, Transepts, Enclosed Choir, Choir
Aisles, Chapels, Chantries, Corona, Libraries, Chapter House,
Crypt and Water Tower, dating from early Saxon to Victorian
Gothic.   But this jumble is the jumble of our own history
since the Cross of Christ was carried on shore at Pegwell
Bay.   To criticise Canterbury is to criticise England, and
make Englishmen annoyed.

I remember my own annoyance when, standing for the
first time at Christ Church Gate, I was joined by a French
bourgeois family on a day trip from Calais.   They fussed up,
jabbering, then waited for hot indignant little " papa " to
voice the family's disgust at being out of France.   He obliged :
" Mais c'est beaucoup moins beau que Notre Dame."
Impertinent insularity—I remember my fury to this day, as
I remember my satisfaction at coming across the following
passage in *Gostling's Walk* : " Entering in company with
some of our colonists just arrived from America . . . how
have I seen the countenances, even of their negroes, sparkle
with rapture of admiration."

In fact, our English pride in Canterbury is not altogether
justified.   The foundations were laid by the Roman missionary,
Augustine, on the site of an earlier Roman church, and
Augustine became Canterbury's first Archbishop and Saint.
The " glorious choir," now the heart of the whole Anglican
Church, was probably the conception of a French mason,

31   Canterbury Cathedral : the Fabric

32   Canterbury Cathedral : the Black Prince's Tomb

33   The Morning Class, King's School, Canterbury

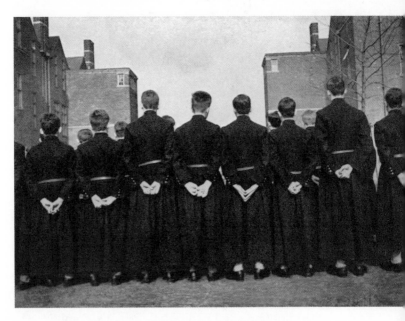

34   Bluecoat Boys, Horsham

William of Sens, and is for the greater part based on the superb cathedral of that town. Historically, the city would have sunk to minor importance but for the assassination in the actual precincts of a truculent priest of French parentage. Previous to this murder (an episode that ranks with the regicide in Sarajevo as an example of how history can be written by any fool's haphazard act), Canterbury had been superseded in importance by the royal city of Westminster, and even Winchester, and was little heard of. It now became Europe's most popular sacred shrine.

For the next three centuries Christians dribbled along the three grassy tracks from London, Winchester and the port of Dover, until they became Pilgrims' Roads; year after year they dribbled up the nave and through the choir aisles until their feet left grooves in the hard Caen stone; day after day the great frescoed wooden canopy was hauled up by unseen ropes, revealing the glittering shrine—all papered with gold leaf, strewn with gold rings, peppered with diamonds, rubies, carbuncles and pearls. In the centre rested " a chest of iron containing the bones of Thomas à Becket, skull and all, with the wounds of his death, and the piece out of his skull. As all fell on their knees, the prior came forward and touched the several jewels with a White Wand, naming the giver of each. One was supposed to be the finest in England. It was a great carbuncle or diamond, as large as a hen's egg, called 'The Regale of France' and presented by Louis VII. of France, who, said the legend, was unwilling to part with so great a treasure; but the stone leapt from the ring in which he wore it, and fastened itself firmly into the shrine — a miracle against which there was no striving " (Stowe and Murray).

Richard Cœur de Lion came here walking barefooted from Sandwich—a distance of twelve miles—to give thanks to St. Thomas for his release from an Austrian prison. Edward I. came to offer the crown of Scotland; Henry V. to thank Becket for his victory at Agincourt. Among distinguished foreign pilgrims were Manuel, Emperor of the East, Sigismund, Emperor of the West, and the Emperor Charles V. of Spain who rode with Henry VIII. from Dover. " Under the same canopy were seen both youthful sovereigns; Cardinal Wolsey was directly in front; on the right and left were the proud nobles of Spain and England . . ." (Stanley).

Eighteen years later Henry VIII. showed a sudden and profitable change of mind. Whatever his faults, one must admire his enlightened disregard of mediæval superstition

F

—even his adoption of it to his own ends. The defunct Becket was charged with treason. For thirty days the summons was read out at his shrine, and when he failed to appear, his case was argued at Westminster. The Attorney-General represented the defunct Henry II. Becket's advocate, an obscure lawyer, lost his case, which was not surprising since he was appointed by Henry VIII. The shrine was dismantled; the saint's bones burnt; the offerings of three hundred and fifty years forfeited to the Crown.

Pilgrims to-day will find little in the Cathedral to remind them of this murder, which was " regarded throughout Christendom as unexampled in sacrilege since the crucifixion of our Lord." Where the shrine stood is now an empty space which visitors ignore in preference for the adjacent tomb of the Black Prince. The " martyrdom " in the recon-structed North Transept has but one small flagstone that guides and school teachers can point out as the spot where Becket fell. And they are almost certainly wrong.

It is easier to-day to reconstruct the scene in the corre-sponding South Transept, which has a similar staircase to the one which staged the fatal brawl. For it was as a brawl that the trouble started. There had been shouting and threatening outside the precincts—half an hour of it—but no harm done. Had Becket now chosen to pacify these over-zealous half-wits, not one, perhaps, would have dared strike the first blow; for how oafish they must have felt, these uncouth soldiers clattering into the dim solemnity of the Cathedral. It was five o'clock on a winter's evening. Vespers were being sung. But Becket, too, was a soldier; he had led troops in battle and, single-handed, unhorsed a celebrated French knight. It was Becket who had unlocked the door from the cloisters crying " the church must not be turned into a castle," and, refusing to hide with his monks, had stood with his back against a pillar to receive Fitzurse, Tracy, le Bret, de Moreville, and a chaplain, Hugh of Horsa, with soldier's abuse. The beginning of the fighting seems to have been only tentative, and Becket succeeded in throwing Tracy to the ground. The first sword-stroke was still half-hearted: Fitzurse knocked off the Archbishop's hat. It was left to Tracy, who had regained his feet, to draw first blood—he half severed the arm of a clerk, Edward Grim, who had attempted to parry a blow at his master's head. Grim now fled and Becket stood alone, a candle-lit figure in white. Back in the gloom of the church, hiding behind their altars, crouched whispering monks. Tracy struck again. . . . It had seemed beyond belief, murder in the sanctuary of his own church! Becket covered his face with his hands and hastily muttered prayers to his God and the saints of Canterbury—Augustine, Blaize, Alphege and Andoen of Rouen. Again Tracy struck. The white figure crashed suddenly, face down. Le Bret shouted, "Take this . . ." and sliced off the crown of the skull. With bravado of fearful guilt the chaplain, Hugh of Horsa, probed the brains with his sword point—scattering them over the placid stones.

V

NORTH OF THE DOWNS TO CHICHESTER

I

FROM Lewes a narrow Saxon road winds westward tucked under the slope of the Downs. There is a welcome feeling of unpopularity attached to this road— it is the cheap hotel bedroom with a northern aspect and no view of the sea. And it has the same cosiness—protected always by this hump of chalk from the south-westerly gales and " Palaces of Fun." It twists in and out among the lowest foothills, and every few miles you find a small church among decrepit yews. Plumpton, Clayton, Pycombe, Poynings, Edburton—they are not of outstanding interest except as being typical of this part of Sussex, with their squat towers or little shingled spires, and steep roofs that slope without clerestory to within a foot or two of the ground.

But the village of Ditchling no longer belongs to this type of Sussex hamlet. Since Eric Gill and Frank Brangwyn chose to live here, every craft—whether stirring jam, weaving stuffs, or printing books—must be done patiently by hand. It is a temptation to joke about village handcrafts. I admit that I visited Mr. Pepler's " St. Dominic's Press " and Miss Mairet's hand-weaving school intending to scoff; but remained to criticise. Not that I have any right to be critical : I would never dream, for instance, of straining my claret through a filter. No matter how efficient a filter science may produce, I shall insist on decanting—even with a shaky hand. Again, when I built on a studio to my mill house, I went to the extravagance of handmade bricks ; here I was actually *relying* on the fallibility of the hand to produce an æsthetic

35   The Way to School across Clayton Downs, Sussex

36 The Castellated House over the Clayton Downs Tunnel
on the Brighton Line

37 Fancy Homes at Fulking, Sussex

patina, and, had I been unable to afford this luxury, I should have relied on nature's weathering. But is it not fortunate that the brickmaker's fallibility should produce a broken pattern to our taste ? Is it not fortunate that we find lichen attractive ? When nature might so well have elected to grow some loathsome fungi instead. And much the same applies to hand printing, weaving and carving, hand-stirred jams, and all other crafts that boast of being "done by hand"; they, too, are relying for their merit on the human error rather than an infallible machine.

The craftsman will no doubt claim that he has greater possibilities of selection, though, in fact, the selectivity of an up-to-date machine (which is, in any case, primarily made and ultimately controlled by hand) can be almost unlimited. Where the machine differs is that its selection is not happy-go-lucky, but precise. With more truth he will argue that a machine leaves no freedom for the creative artist. But supposing the artist were to create the machine ? We cannot expect every hand printer to have Mr. Pepler's distinctive gifts; surely it is the duty of men with such gifts to go to the spring-head. Then, having first purified the huge industrial flow, they might inundate and sweep away all the muck now protected under the label of " arts and crafts."

There is one real objection to all this ; the Peplers would probably work in vain—industry is not over-interested in perfection except when it is essential, as in the manufacture of lethal weapons and fighter-aircraft—but they could make the effort, and how much more worth-while even an effort would be than the little precious outcrop which is all they now achieve. Think of a world in which every single brick was perfection and every page of every book and newspaper and magazine. *Only* by machinery can this be achieved. Then we'll hide away our hand-made luxuries, for they will look just as shoddy—even as ornaments—as a hand-forged medi-æval musket beside the rifled barrel of a naval gun.

II

The village of Clayton, too, has something else of interest beside its church—a fine double " Folly " called the Tunnel House. Should you have to spend a night in a railway hotel, think of this " Folly " and sleep with relief. Trains do not go past the house but right through the middle, so that the front is blackened with smoke. To have designed the entrance of a tunnel as a railwayman's cottage—that was folly. To have designed the cottage as a Tudor castellated fortress was mad.

The road winds on to Steyning, which was once a harbour, and Bramber, the fortress that guarded the entrance of the creek. To-day the cliffs rise from green fields, and of Bramber castle there remains only sufficient ruins to persuade tourists to climb the steep hill. " The wealth of primroses," described in *Murray's Handbook* of 1903, have disappeared with their roots.

In the main street of the village is a rival attraction to the ruin in Potter's Museum, which represents the seventy years' labour of a Bramber " Surrealist," Walter Potter (1835–1918). Some advanced London gallery might well exhibit his work— both his original constructions and his " objets trouvés." Of the former I recommend : " The Upper Ten. Consisting of twenty-one red squirrels, some of which are drinking and smoking, while others are engrossed in a debate " ; the fifteenth-century iron treasure-chest containing a litter of stuffed foxes ; the monkey riding a goat ; and " The Guinea-Pigs' Cricket Match. This case contains thirty-four of these favourite little animals." (*Sic.*)

It would take some weeks to sort out the " objets trouvés " —cheek by jowl in glass cases, is crowded the most incongruous assortment ever collected under one roof. I select from the catalogue, choosing at random : Brazil nuts ; a blunderbuss ; a dog fish " with attachment " ; a coconut ; the first time-table issued between Brighton and Partridge Green ; a kitten with three faces, two eyes, two noses and two mouths ; a model of a church made entirely of feathers, quills and pins ; a Louis XVI. banknote (promising " il sera payé au porteur la somme de cinq cents livres ") ; a jawbone of an ass ; a Mersey tunnel 1s. 6d. toll ticket of 1934 ; an old copy of *The Times* ; another cat with eight legs and two tails ; and a photograph of some top-hatted Bechuanaland chiefs who once paid a visit to this remarkable museum.

In contrast, sightseeing in the neighbouring village of Steyning seems a prosaic business, unless we recall the origin of the church : it was founded by a shepherd, Cuthman, who came from the West of England. As a boy he discovered that, when he wished to play truant, he had only to draw a circle with his crook round his father's flock and command the sheep to remain within the ring until his return. One would have thought that Cuthman's future as a shepherd was assured, but, on the death of his father, the boy was reduced to begging his way through the country, dragging his invalid mother behind

38   The Village Street, Steyning, Sussex

39   Wiston Park and Chanctonbury Ring in the Sussex Downs

him in a home-made barrow. When the cords wore out he replaced them with branches from an elderberry tree. Some haymakers standing by mocked him, and for ever after a heavy local shower fell on their field at the time the hay was mown. When at last the branches gave way, Cuthman decided that his begging days were over ; he built a hut for his unfortunate old mother and a small wooden church in gratitude for his successful journey. During building, a beam of the church became dislodged, so that the whole edifice was in danger of collapse. At that moment a stranger appeared and showed the amateur architect how to put the damage right. Cuthman thanked him and asked him who he was. " I am He," the stranger replied, " in Whose name thou buildest this temple."

This legend brought many pilgrims to Saint Cuthman's church, and the town of Steyning grew up around it. Many years later, Edward the Confessor granted Steyning to the Benedictines of Fécamp—the wooden church was replaced by an abbey of stone. Through this gift Steyning played an indirect but memorable part in English history ; for King Harold's repudiation of the gift was, to a great extent, responsible for William of Normandy's decision to invade our shores.

The present church is only a fragment of the original, but the nave remains as an example of how all æsthetic movements become debased in their final dying effort to survive. The early Norman chancel arch—forty feet high—is superb, and its narrow zigzag pattern springing from scolloped capitals, enrichment inspired. In contrast, the stubby, over-decorated arches of the nave seem but a last vulgar Benedictine gesture ; they were carved in 1180, when the elegant pointed arch of the Cistercians was on its way.

III

Just outside the town a thick-skinned traveller can take a short cut to the main Arundel road—one of those nerve-racking short cuts that follow a very private-looking gravel drive through a very private park. This particular road (I hope I am right in assuming that it is a public way) calls for more than normal daring since it sweeps up to, and past, the very door of Wiston House, and one imagines the family gathering up their books prior to flight into a back room, while the butler crosses the hall with measured tread and shooting cuffs. But it is worth all embarrassment to gain a close view of this grey Elizabethan house, which has a setting as classical as a Poussin landscape, with its park falling smoothly down to a lake, and at the back a high pinnacle of down crowned by a symmetrical clump of beeches.

This clump—an eighteenth-century Folly—is the responsibility of Charles Goring, a former owner of the house, who, with his own hands, planted each tree as a twig, and, for the rest of his long life, climbed almost daily to the summit to check their growth. The trees were full-grown before he died, and he was permitted to see for himself to what extent his solitary, conspicuous landmark had transformed every panorama viewed from thirty miles around. But even then he was probably unaware of the full consequences of his experiment ; for these beeches have now sown themselves from Petworth to Arundel, changing—and I think beautifying—the whole character of the Downs. And surely no man has been responsible for so many exhausted tourists as Charles Goring. Standing on Leith Hill or Box Hill, Mount Harry or The Devil's Dyke, they point out this landmark with triumph : triumphant they are at their superior topographical knowledge ; triumphant at having found so fine a panoramic view. " Look," they cry, " there's old Chanctonbury Ring." But sooner or later they can resist no longer ; it becomes an obsession ; they must climb those seven hundred feet to the summit. I only succumbed after eleven years.

It is a tedious enough climb, even by the chalk track that ascends with consideration from contour to contour along the northern slope of the down ; but the return journey is less pleasant still—a precipitous descent—for who can resist the temptation to plunge directly down the sheer hillside to their car just below ? Nevertheless I was glad to have succumbed, for without doubt there is a certain satisfaction in eliminating from the system a persistent curiosity. I had gazed at Chanctonbury Ring long enough ; it was time I found out what was there.

Alongside the eighteenth-century Folly I discovered an eighteenth-century dew pond ; both singularly out of place on this remote plateau that overlooks ridge after ridge of a prehistoric landscape, and has no other mark on its smooth miles of turf except the straight impression of a track left by prehistoric man. Then I discovered the " Ring " of Chanctonbury, which was not, as I had always supposed, Goring's clump of beeches, but a circular depression hidden within the wood— the trench and rampart of a prehistoric camp. And it is round this circle that you must run three times at midnight if you wish to see the Devil appear to offer you porridge from his bowl.

IV

Until the opening of the railway Arundel was a flourishing port. To-day, though the Arun can be navigated by boats of three hundred tons, it is only pleasure-craft that come to moor by the old bridge. From the bridge the main street slopes steeply to the castle gates. It is a beautiful street ; most of the shops—the chemist, the ladies' hairdresser, the creamery, the tea parlours and cafés (even " Honey Buns ")—are eighteenth-century perfection. But it is the castle that dominates this small town visually and morally ; wherever you look and whatever you do, there is no escape from this castellation that crowns the hill.

Visually the building is a complete success—though Americans should be warned that it is not fifty per cent. antique. During the Civil War, Sir W. Waller, commanding the Parliamentary troops, placed his cannon on the church tower and for seventeen days lobbed round shot into the castle from point-blank range. It surrendered as a ruin. There was no attempt to rebuild until a hundred years later, when the eighth Duke of Norfolk made a small portion habitable ; but it was not until 1790 that the tenth Duke, acting as his own architect, created this Wagnerian fantasy that might have caused envy in the heart of mad Ludwig II.

A symbol of the moral domination of the castle is to be found in the parish church : a rough brick wall, built by a Duke of Norfolk to shut off the chancel from the nave. The vicar of the parish pulled the wall down, and there followed in 1878 the famous trial: " The Duke of Norfolk *versus* Rev. G. Arbuthnot."

" This is an act of trespass "—so began Lord Justice Coleridge in his summing up—" for breaking down a wall built on the plaintiff's land. The defendant is the vicar of the parish of Arundel, and he pleads, in substance, that the wall was built so as to obstruct his right of entrance into the chancel of his church, and to prevent the passage of light and air from the chancel to the church, and that he broke down the wall because it obstructed and interfered with his rights. . . ."

After some ten thousand more words on the history of the church and Fitzalan family, he gave judgment for the Duke of Norfolk for forty shillings damages and costs. To-day visitors, who are curious to see the other side of this wall, must make a quarter-mile detour through the lodge gate and buy a sixpenny ticket to view " the Fitzalan chapel "—once the chancel of this parish church. That I am reticent about this chapel, which contains eight monuments and twenty brasses, is not through pique or thrift. The domination of the castle was too strong for me ; having walked the quarter-mile and paid my sixpenny fine, I was told by the guide that I must not write in my notebook without permission, nor—since the family were in residence—must I " hang around."

Perhaps I should attempt to describe these tombs from memory—these husbands and wives that lie in effigy of dark Purbeck marble, new white marble, alabaster, or Caen stone ; but memory can be over-selective : only one tomb can I see in detail, the tomb of John Fitzalan, who died of wounds and was buried at Beauvais in 1435. He rests in his armour with his war horse at his feet—it is a beautiful but conventional symbol of the glory of a knight's death. In the lower half of the tomb lies a similar effigy ; it depicts John Fitzalan as he returned to his home on the Arun. Surely the sculptor must have witnessed the return—he must have *seen* this sunk-in corpse with its cape of satin, and skull crowned like a debutante with a tuft of ostrich plumes.

Originally the church formed part of a college of Sacré priests, founded in the fourteenth century by Richard Fitzalan, thirteenth earl of Arundel. He was beheaded in 1397 by Richard II. There followed a pilgrimage to the Augustinian church in Cheapside, where he was buried. Eventually it was rumoured that a miracle had taken place, in that body and head had become reunited. Richard II. became so perturbed by the increasing number of pilgrims that he had the grave opened. As the parish guidebook puts it, " nothing extraordinary was found."

V

To the north of Arundel a green track can be traced that cuts a straight line through the beech woods and across the downs above the village of Bignor. The track is Stane Street, once the Roman highway from Chichester to London. At the side of this highway there stood a luxury villa—the home, probably, of the local Roman governor. The buildings with court-yard, stables and baths covered three or four acres. Just as the great mansions of the 'eighties, now schools or demolished for their breakdown value, were looked on as the family seats

40   The View from the Devil's Dyke, looking to Chanctonbury, Sussex

41 The Palladian Pavilion in Goodwood Park, Sussex, giving views over the Solent

of generations to come, so this palace must have seemed a home built to last for ever. Then, to defend their own country, the Roman Legions were recalled. It was only for a few months —so the caretaker was told—but year followed year, while the Romanised Britons sent messages " with their tears " pleading with the great Empire to return and protect them from the Saxons, the Picts and the Scots, and the Viking pirates from the North Sea.

The great Empire had crumbled ; and so crumbled the walls of the luxury villa, until, in the course of time, looting and wild nature destroyed all traces. This Roman governor and his great importance were forgotten when—fifteen hundred years later—a Sussex yokel sent up a shower of small mosaics with the blade of his plough. The foundations of the villa were excavated, and to-day we can follow the ground plan of the house from its pavements, central heating pipes, and mosaiced floors. The red, black, and white mosaics, protected during the centuries by two feet of soil, look almost new, and in many rooms the design is intact—though the term " design " is flattering to these conventional geometrical patterns that might come from a Victorian oilcloth. One wonders whether early Britons passing along Stane Street ever complained about the new eyesore in their forest landscape—this luxury villa in the very worst taste.

VI

The Downs between Bignor and the borders of Hampshire should be aimlessly explored. This is a landscape that is for ever changing with each bend of the road : you may find high forests of pale young beeches or a barren hillside neatly dotted with dark clumps of ilex and yew ; smooth slopes with cattle grazing, or great squares of ploughland dazzling white. And from the high ground the sea is the horizon, rising and falling behind the grey needle of Chichester Cathedral spire. There are no great main roads to the West ; you can follow the snug valley of the Lavant through East and West Dean, contented little villages that have no need to worry whether the wind blows from the sea or the land. Or you can find your way through Saxon lanes to Cocking ; in the church is a fresco that should appeal to dog lovers—a fresco of naïf charm. An angel has appeared to two shepherds, who are regarding this unusual apparition with conventional Biblical calm ; but when it came to portraying their dog, the artist seems to have considered that his licence had expired : this mongrel is shown straining at his collar, standing on his hind legs, and yapping, yapping, yapping just as fiendishly as mongrels yap to-day.

Having reached Cocking, probably with difficulty, don't be tempted by the main road all the way into Chichester—sacrifice speed for the steep hill that goes slap over the crest of the downs past Trundle Camp. Trundle, with Whitehawk above Brighton, is one of the earliest British encampments in Sussex ; together they have provided archæologists with their surest knowledge of the uncouth life led by our cannibal ancestors in their pits on the top of the downs. But Trundle, like White-hawk, adjoins a racecourse, and whatever romantic thoughts these sites might conjure, are minimised by so close a view of the Silver Ring.

Half a mile down the southern slope of Goodwood Park, hidden by a grove of beeches, stands a little classical Pavilion. Though sharing the same view, it is the extreme antithesis of the pit dwellings on the hill above. This is a building for pleasure pure and simple ; an eighteenth-century summer-house, guarded by two sphinxes, with a great window looking across untilled park land to the sea ; it is surely one of the most beautiful examples of luxury architecture to be found in England.

A few yards from the Pavilion, among the trees, is an eighteenth-century Folly that has almost as much charm : a shell room built by the second Duchess of Richmond and her daughters with their own hands. The walls are an entrancing mosaic of coloured shells, with mirrors inlaid ; the floor is paved with a pattern of horses' teeth—it is not surprising that this grotto took these women seven years to complete. The origin of the Folly is unexpected : it was built " in memory of a valued friend," Carne, who was tutor to the daughters— what a charmer he must have been ! One likes to think of the stately duchess dragging her daughters up the hill—weather wet or fine ; their expeditions to the seashore in search of material ; the carefully drawn, tinted designs. For seven years her aristocratic fingers puddled liquid mortar, scrubbed each shell and cleaned each horse's tooth—seven years' labour to erect her little memorial in this secluded place. Was this Folly, one wonders, literally " une folie d'amour "—literally, a labour of love ?

In the central mirror of the grotto is reflected the spire of Chichester Cathedral. It is comparatively modern, having replaced the ancient Gothic spire in 1862. In my Foreword I have promised the reader not to dwell in detail on cathedral architecture—Chichester, in particular, I agreed to leave out.

43 Restoration Plaster Ceiling in the Church of
King Charles the Martyr, Tunbridge Wells

42 The Shell Grotto in Goodwood Park,
Sussex

44 Bosham Village and Creek, West Sussex

45 The Inn at Blackboys, near Uckfield, Sussex

But there is a story about the original spire which seems worth repeating—it used to be told by my aunt, the late Countess of Wemyss. When a child, she was travelling down to Chichester by train ; it was her first visit, and, as they approached the city, her mother said, " Look, darling, there's the Cathedral." She looked out of the carriage window to see the spire fall down.

VI

ACROSS THE WEALD INTO SURREY

I

AS far as I am concerned, Haywards Heath means an electrified, fifty-minute train service to London; the road from Blackboys to the station, a series of hairpin corners deliberately planned by the Saxons so that their more civilised descendant should miss his train. If you are not bound for the station you can avoid some of the horror of Haywards Heath by slipping off to the right past Lindfield's five-acre green and the duckpond which is now graced by a pair of swans. But stop a moment in the charming village—if the hour is at all reasonable, stop for Sussex's regional dish; at the Pent Arms Hotel the bacon and eggs are only equalled on the " Brighton Belle." The street of alternating black-and-white half-timbered cottages, and Georgian fronts of bow-windowed brick, slopes up to the church between pollarded plane trees and limes. The church has been stripped of all interest—even the fourteenth-century frescoes have been scrubbed clean away. Beyond the churchyard stand three houses : a seventeenth-century half-timbered brick farmhouse, now a show piece with its iron grille, lawns and trimmed yews ; and, facing each other, two Queen Anne brick houses—show places since the first scaffolding was removed.

If you have time for a walk, take the footpath from the church to the famous half-timbered farm of Mascalls, and on the way you will pass another farm, Little Walstead, never restored—a complete example of a yeoman's house as it was three hundred years ago.

Cuckfield is not unlike Lindfield—it has the same steep sloping street and patchwork of façades. But the church is at the foot of the hill, and so screened by the Council School and

46   Little Walstead Farm, near Lindfield, Sussex

48 Tennyson's Home : Aldworth House, Blackdown, Sussex

47 The Tudor Ruins of Cowdray, Sussex

King's Head Hotel that you can pass it without even seeing the spire. From the churchyard there is a view that could only be Sussex; ridges of hedged fields, small copses of chestnut and oak, a twisting line of alder marking a hidden stream, and, as a backcloth, the flat painted silhouette of the downs, crowned by two windmills—one black and one white—which are known locally as Jack and Jill.

In contrast, the pleasantly gaudy interior of the church is reminiscent of Bavaria. The whole ceiling, with its beams and bosses, the chancel arches, and the organ pipes have been painted by Kempe in scarlet and blue and gold; the walls are enriched by over thirty monuments, mostly coloured. There are tombs by Flaxman and Ady and Westmacott; and a lovely seventeenth-century group " To the memorie of that worthy young gentleman Ninian Burrell "—in which the kneeling figure and two angels have all the gay freedom of Baroque.

Many of these monuments belong to the Sergison family who lived in the Elizabethan manor, Cuckfield Place—better known in fiction as " Rookwood Hall." On our road to Cowfold we pass the gates and glimpse the house through an avenue of limes. This momentary view is not reassuring; in fact, I have always assumed the building to be Victorian from foundation to roof.

Cowfold is another village that hides its lamp under a bushel. Year after year I have concentrated on the dangerous double bend and cross-roads, and—but for this book—should have never realised that in the church, behind the insignificant row of shops, was one of the most spectacular brasses in all England. Ten feet in length, it covers the tomb of Thomas Nelond, a Cluniac monk who was in charge of Lewes Priory at the beginning of the fifteenth century. He is shown standing under a triple canopy, his hands clasped in prayer. The central arch of the canopy encloses a chapel in which are seated the Holy Virgin and Child. On either side stand St. Pancras, Patron Saint of Lewes, and St. Thomas à Becket. Perhaps I should warn the reader that it costs a shilling to view.

II

To the north of Cowfold there stretches a series of forests (at least so they are called on the map) : St. Leonard's, Tilgate, Balcombe and Worth. St. Leonard's is a forest of legendary error, but to-day these hundreds of acres are cut through by

the London-Brighton road, and their aspect is everywhere reassuring. How many city men, returning late from a Brighton
week-end, realise that a headless phantom may spring on to
their luggage carrier and refuse to be dislodged until the
boundaries of the forest are passed ? What is it to a hiker
should he one day meet face to face " a strange monstrous ser-
pent or dragon . . . living to the great annoyance and diverse
slaughters both of men and cattle " ? What is it but " silly
season " front-page news ? And the sweaty, head-bowed string
of cyclists, with their fresh-rooted lilies of the valley tied dying
to the handle-bars—do they care that these blooms have
flowered from the sprinkled blood-drops of St. Leonard, who
fought for many days with yet another " mighty worm " ?
Perhaps no one will miss the song of the nightingale ; perhaps
no one minds that these birds may never again sing within the
precincts of St. Leonard's Forest, having been cursed by a
hermit whom they disturbed in his cell.

Even if you leave the highway and strike an adventurous
path—there is little hope of adventure ; Nature and man
between them have left no cover for headless monsters and
mighty worms. Nature in a great storm destroyed the grim
oaks ; in their stead man has planted rows of silly Christmas
trees. In any case you cannot travel far ; notice-boards stop
that, and little properties bounded by creosoted fencing or
trimmed privet hedges. The old hammer ponds are now ornamental lakes, but only barbed wire prevented me trespassing
in search of fresh-water mussels to be found on the banks.
" Crow mussels " they are called, being considered a delicacy
by the carrion crow. But were I proprietor I would at least
try a " soupe aux moules."

The forest of Worth is more impressive, though the trees
are still small, having replaced the oaks that fell during the
plundering of the Weald. Along the road are boards offering
plots for sale—so these trees, too, must die before they reach
their prime. North of the forest is the church of Worth. It
stands a mile and a half from the village, alone in a grove of
trees. To the archæologist this is, perhaps, the most important
of small Sussex churches—without doubt it is one of the most
beautiful. I shall make no attempt to describe the twelfth-
century double font, the sixteenth-century carved pulpit
brought from the German town of Worth, the musicians'
gallery which was the gift of a rector in 1610, nor the seventeenth-century altar rails, candelabrum and Sanctuary chairs.
I do not care whether the nave and chancel date from the time
of Ethelred the Second or Edward the Confessor—the only

one thing I saw was the grey ghostly arch between them—and
that is the only thing that I will remember. For this colossal
Saxon arch seems to combine all the awe of paganism with the
courage of the first dawn of Christian belief.

III

On our road to Horsham we pass within a mile or two of the
hamlet of Slaugham. The three acres of ruins which lie below
the church, in the valley of the Ouse, mark the site of Slaugham
Place, one of the largest English mansions ever built. It was
the home of the Coverts, to whom a house of size seems to
have been a necessity ; they were a quick-breeding family ; at
one period, according to Horsfield, seventy members lived
here under the same roof. To cater for so many required
ingenuity—special water conduits were constructed, and a
staff of mechanics lived permanently in the house. To-day the
roof has disappeared, and all trace of the building except some
arches, pillars and stone walls which have been transformed
into one of the loveliest gardens I know.

In the church are the family monuments, including the much-
eulogised Richard Covert memorial—he is shown with his
three wives. This ornate work in marble was, no doubt,
ordered regardless of expense, for the price has actually been
recorded : thirty pounds—a considerable sum in the sixteenth
century. Never of great beauty, it was drastically restored in
the 'eighties " by the hands (*sic*) of the Rev. William Haweis."
There is a photograph of the restorer in the vestry. In appearance he must have modelled himself on Tennyson—he is
indistinguishable from the Poet Laureate. How well one can
imagine the clergyman's adoration of the great Victorian, who
had come to this tiny parish to pass the first year of his married
life.

Tennyson was already famous when he came to live here in
1851 (at the age of forty he had received his Laureateship)—but
penniless, having been swindled out of all his property and
money by a bogus firm, " The Patent Decorative Carving
Company." His cottage at Warninglid was worse than humble
—it was a hovel ; within a few months a wall collapsed.
Tennyson left Sussex in disgust. But seventeen years later he
returned to build himself " Aldworth," a Gothic Revival
mansion on Blackdown—the highest point of Sussex, on the
sandy forest ridge.

Blackdown is well named ; its plantations of gloomy conifers rise in black silhouette from the Weald.   A footpath circles the crest, labelled " Tennyson's Walk."   To what extent, one wonders, did the man impose his mood on this countryside ? Or did he find here awaiting him a landscape that could echo his poems ?   There is no telling ; but this hilltop might have been planted by God as a last retreat for a great Victorian poet ;   so mournful a barrenness might strike terror, but for the wellingtonia and rhododendrons, and the larches framing the prehistoric views.

I had an opportunity this summer of visiting the house, through the kindness of " The Poetry Society."   They were holding a recital of poems spoken by Tennyson himself—in 1889 Edison recorded the poet's voice.   The house is now empty; we sat on the staircase or on hired gilt chairs—loud-speakers relayed to every room.   A " Punch and Judy " sound was to be expected; the recording had to be done through a mouthpiece when Tennyson was eighty years old—after which the records had lain undiscovered for thirty-five years; they then had to be recast in metal before being transferred from the phonograph cylinders on to gramophone discs.   Neverthe-less, the poet's peculiar technique was clear : most noticeable was his emotional underlining of the rhythm and changes of tempo.   I remember as a child being embarrassed by Victorians reading poetry after dinner : the unashamed emotion with which they read—young girls quavering senility ;   old men wiping imaginary tears as they piped a maiden's part.   I was embarrassed because I wanted to giggle.   I now realised that this must have been the fashion of the period.   Tennyson started off " The Charge of the Heavy Brigade " at full gallop— the lines became onomatopœic—and he did not draw breath until " Up the hill, up—the—hill, up——the——hill " ; it grew steeper and steeper.   At the end of each verse, the voice sank until barely audible ; eternity seemed to elapse between each word : " Followed . . . the . . . Heavy . . . Brigade."

It was raining when I left.   I walked on to the terrace where he used to sit and look with failing eyes across the Weald. The fir trees dripped on the soggy lawn ;   mists of fine rain drifted across the famous view—I could not even see the vale below me.   Only a poet could have brought summer back to this sad prospect :

> " *As this red rose which on our terrace here*
> *Glows in the blue of fifty miles away.*"

The lines pierced the mist as light through an amber screen.

49 A Heath on Ashdown Forest, near King's Standing, Sussex

50 The Balcombe Railway Viaduct on the Brighton Line

IV

The beauty of the overpopulated English landscape must depend more often than not on the house-tops. Sussex has been fortunate in having three materials with which to vary her roofs and spires : wooden shingles from the forest weald, tiles from the clay, and, near Horsham, slabs of stone. Walking in this part of Sussex you may find a Horsham stone quarry in any out-of-the-way field : a slice removed from the middle of the field, exposing symmetrical layers of clay and stone like a sandwich cake. The stone comes out in natural flat slabs, ready for use, but of varying thickness. This thickness cannot be changed, so that at one period a quarry will produce slates for roofing, at another only crazy paving. Except for repair work, there is little call nowadays for roofing stone—the modern villa cannot support the weight. But every old roof in this landscape—cottage, church, farmhouse and mansion—as well as every footpath that runs between, are laid with this beautiful grey lichened stone.

Horsham, which is the capital of West Sussex, is the type of town one connects with hunt balls held in a draughty Corn Exchange, old coaching inns now " Trust Houses," and a long narrow High Street where the county comes shopping in liveried chauffeur-driven old limousines. In fact, Horsham would be the typical English provincial town, were it not for small boys who walk the streets dressed in mediæval costume— a long dark blue coat, dark blue breeches, white " stands " like starched bibs, and mustard-coloured stockings. They are newcomers to the town—these Blue Coat boys ; Newgate was their place of origin, where Edward VI. founded Christ's Hospital School in 1552 for the sons of the unwealthy. After the Fire of London, Christopher Wren rebuilt the school, but at the beginning of this century it was demolished, and, on the high ground south of Horsham, Sir Aston Webb erected ten acres of brick blocks in the Tudor Style.

I had left Horsham, and was on my way to Itchingfield, when I caught sight of the tower and buildings. There is no difficulty in getting a permit to view, and these schoolboys show unusual consideration and good manners to a visitor ; during the lunch hour I was allowed to wander among the tables, peering at the food and taking photographs, without receiving one jibe or stare.

Of the original building a few mementoes have been transported to Sussex—that is the most one can call these treasures that have survived. In the dining-room we find a carved pulpit, and a canvas by Antonio Verrio that must be sixty feet long, showing Charles II. at the founding of Wren's building. Above the daïs in the speech room is a superb golden-piped organ ; in a niche over the entrance a Grinling Gibbons statue of Sir John Moore. At the back of this building, forming part of the wall, stands Wren's original gateway with a gilded statue of Edward VI.

Though the shell has changed, the school tradition remains unaltered : the boys' costume has hardly varied since the sixteenth century ; on St. Matthew's Day the school still attends a service in Christ Church, Newgate, and each boy receives from the Lord Mayor a shilling, rising to a guinea for " First Parting Grecians." The fees are low and on a scale according to parents' means ; but these eight hundred boys receive an education as good as in any English public school. Coleridge was taught here, Charles Lamb and Leigh Hunt ; the three appear together in an unpleasant stained-glass window in the south wall of the chapel. Round the nave of this chapel sixteen panels by Brangwyn are ill placed. Done in tempera, they give the impression of frescoes—but frescoes painted impossibly direct on to brick. But whatever the medium, Brangwyn's ochres and reds would always find uncomfortable quarters on their geranium background supplied by Sir Aston Webb.

For contrast, drive on a mile to the pre-Conquest church of Itchingfield, which stands quite hidden in a grove of cedars and yews. The little tower, with its buttresses, windows and belfry, is constructed entirely out of wood. Primitive as it appears, this tower is not the oldest part of the church ; it was built in the fifteenth century, while a portion of the nave dates from Saxon times. But only a very small portion ; in 1865 the Incorporated Society for Building Churches granted £25 towards restoring and reseating. They employed Sir Gilbert Scott. He pulled down the southern Saxon wall, removed the gallery, and added an aisle to seat seventy extra people. Compared with present-day building prices, £25 seems a small contribution to a leading architect for so much work.

In the churchyard is a toy-like building of half timbering and brick which is now used as a vestry. When the church belonged to Sele Priory this was the priest's house ; a monk would ride over through the forest and sleep the night here before saying mass at dawn.

51 A Cobbled Street at Petworth, Sussex

52   Wiston Park

53   The Stables at Petworth House

Great Sussex Houses

54   Harting Downs, Sussex

55 South Harting, Sussex, under the South Downs

56 The Saxon Church at Sompting, Sussex

V

Turning south we cross Stane Street—the Roman road from Chichester to London—at Billingshurst; a name curiously linked to London's fish market, Billingsgate, which was the terminus of the road. It is disputed whether the names are derived from the great Saxon tribe of Billing or the great Roman road constructor Belinus.

At Wisborough Green the landscape changes. This is West Sussex—heavily wooded, quite unspoilt, as beautiful as any county in England; it is guarded for a few more years from speculative building by the preservation of game. In the church, on the south pier of the chancel arch, are two well-preserved thirteenth-century frescoes, framed in a recessed arch. It is almost certain that a similar painted recess exists beneath the plaster on the north pier—this the vicar demonstrated by tapping the hollow wall. The question of uncovering it, he told me, has been discussed for many years— " But," he pointed out, " what an awful ass I'd look if we made a beastly mess and found nothing there."

Six main roads converge to meet in Petworth—it seems that no minute elapses without two or three green streamlined buses ticking over in the town's little square. But, under the protection of a great house, Petworth remains a sleepy place, and a bus passenger alights to find a statue of William III. in a niche above his head and, for the bus company's booking office, an eighteenth-century house with pediment, *œil-de-bœuf*, portico and fanlight, painted in rich black on a cream façade.

To the private-car owner the town is all wall; a fifteen-foot curving stone wall that makes every corner blind and, at moments, threatens to crush the driver against the houses on the opposite side of the street. North and south of the town it careers off into the country to enclose a park fourteen miles round. Behind this wall stands Petworth House; you pass the main entrance on leaving the village—a classical lodge gate of charm, which carries on each post Gog and Magog, two surrealist faceless figures in armour. As this is one of the largest and most beautiful country houses in England, it is astonishing that the name of the architect, who must have been a Frenchman, should be unknown.

Do not be put off by the unpleasant exterior of the church with its nineteenth-century stucco spire. Inside there are

I

things of interest and of beauty to be seen : of beauty, a Flaxman monument to John Wickins, now skied in the north-east corner of the chancel, and in the south chantry a small alabaster medallion of mother and child.   Of interest, but without beauty (the sculptor boasts that he was never trained), is the monument to the Percy family, erected to his ancestors by George O'Brien, first Earl of Egmont, in his eighty-sixth year.

The Dawtrey memorial in the north chantry, which has been recently coloured in blue and scarlet, silver and gold, combines both interest and beauty.   The two figures, Sir John Dawtrey and his wife, are shown kneeling on prayer-stools under a Perpendicular canopy extravagantly carved and set with coats-of-arms.   In front of each is an open Bible.   Sir John is in armour and his helmet rests on the book.   The helmet that hangs from a nail above the tomb is similar, but with one great difference : it is a tilting helmet, and the front is prudently sealed.

The unusual interest of this monument is that the restoration and repainting have been done by the handy man—a sailor. Particulars are given in the Parish Magazine of February 1935, from which I quote : " A gleam of colour has been added to the Dawtrey tomb in the chapel of St. Thomas with the full approval of the head of the family and, of course, with the consent of Lord Leconfield, to whom this chapel belongs. . . . The work is a labour of love on the part of Commander D. Roe, R.N., who has for many years made a special study of Heraldry, and it is a matter of regret that he had to rejoin his ship before mending the broken hand and ornamental stone rose and putting in final touches to the colouring."

That was four years ago—a long voyage.   When will Commander Roe return to paint over those hands that now look as if they were dressed in white kid gloves ?   Before long, I hope, because (and it is this that is curious) the sailor's repaint-ing is a complete success.

Petworth makes the perfect sightseer's centre ; there is a comfortable Trust House, the necessary shops and a cinema —and what is more enjoyable than sitting alone through an old slapstick English film in a quiet country town ?   For strollers, Lord Leconfield generously provides his park of two thousand acres ; for those with more energy, I can recommend the cross-country walk to the ruins of Cowdray House, following the valley of the Rother which, though only a few hundred yards to the south, remains for ever out of sight of the main Petworth-Midhurst road.   You start along this road for half a mile, then take the first footpath that leads south, crossing the river at Rotherbridge Farm.

From now on I must leave you to pick your own route from the Ordnance map. There are numerous paths and tracks—some public, some doubtful, some leading somewhere, others dead ends. You can walk through meadows by the meandering Rother; or in the woods on the hills beyond, choosing long straight drives through pine copses or rutted tracks in bracken under oaks. You will come across deep shaded pools; and perhaps a solitary farmhouse—passing it with such envy that you consider for a moment giving up all friends and parties to lead a hermit's life. You will get lost often enough—may leave a shoe in a bog of clay; perhaps you will be caught trespassing by a gamekeeper—even peppered during a pheasant drive. But if all these misfortunes should occur on the same morning you will still agree that this is the perfect short walk. And as in all perfect walks there is an inn half-way at Selham, "The Three Moles," in memory of three white moles unearthed during building. Can white moles bring luck? So it seemed: I now came upon that other essential of the perfect cross-country walk—a discovery. I discovered Selham Church, a minute square towerless building that I had passed by during years of ignorance on the road a mile to the north.

From the outside, so small and primitive a church could not be expected to offer more than some fragments of a Saxon arch. But I found this Saxon arch resting on two capitals carved with a Byzantine vision that seemed almost aggressive in this austere little box. On the southern capital, as a symbol of eternity, two snake-like serpents are devouring each other; above is an entwined leaf pattern, and above that a motive of twisted ropes which changes as in a nightmare into twisted strange beasts of neither land nor sea. The other capital is not representative, but perhaps more beautiful; the upper half consists of a basket-work design which Harrison in his *Notes on Sussex Churches* compares to "Solomon's Knot," a symbolic ornamentation among the Comascine Guild of Lake Como. It has been suggested that these capitals were cut by Saxon workmen under Norman supervision. I felt that they were the work of an individual artist who, through his crudeness, was the better able to express his art.

A mile on, at the little inn of South Ambersham, you can eat bread and cheese in a garden and drink bitter from the wood, then recross the Rother by the old humpbacked bridge and turn left past Moore's farm, along a road marked

" Private," into Cowdray Park. Out of sight of the golfers and the Victorian baronial jumble, which is new Cowdray House, there are still to be found oak glades and avenues of chestnut little changed since Queen Elizabeth shot " from a sylvan bower." Half tame, half timid little animals blend with the bracken—descendants of the " three or four deer " that fell centuries ago to the Queen's crossbow.

Deep in a hollow, a mirage among the evening mists of the Rother, stands a mullioned skeleton : the burnt-out ruin of old Cowdray House. It was here that in 1591 the Queen was fêted by the second Viscount Montagu. Her visit was a favour in return for the old man's loyalty during the Armada crisis—in spite of his age he joined up. It appears to have been an expensive favour for the host ; at one meal he had to provide three oxen and over a hundred geese.

The house was burned in 1793—a long-delayed fulfilment of a curse. That was in the reign of Henry VIII., when the first earl seized Battle Abbey with the King's approval. The last monk to leave came up to him and prophesied : " By fire and water thy line shall come to an end and it shall perish out of the land." While Cowdray was still smouldering, the last Lord Montagu was planning to shoot the falls of the Rhine at Lauffen. He was drowned. And his two remaining heirs— sons of his sister, Mrs. Poyntz—they too were drowned, a year or two later, bathing at Bognor. After this, the house was sold by Mr. Poyntz to the Earl of Egmont, but no attempt was made to restore its magnificence. To-day the grounds are kept rolled and mown by the Midhurst Sports Club. Of old Cowdray House there is nothing left to see but a charred romantic silhouette standing among a grove of goal-posts.

These ruins are the end of our walk. In Midhurst, across the river, by the great iron gates, is the bus stop. Buses to Petworth leave at the half-hour.

VI

Rogate is the last Sussex village on this road. A mile or two on is the border of Hampshire, or, by turning right at the cross-roads near the church, we can be in Surrey within a few minutes. Surrey is our goal ; but first let us turn down the opposite lane into South Harting, an agreeable elongated village street under the beech-clad slope of the Harting Downs. On this slope stands a square red-brick house, Up Park, built about 1685 by Talman, the architect of Chatsworth. On the

57   Farm Buildings near Buxted, Sussex

58   The Rolling Team, Udimore, Sussex

59   The " Long Man of Wilmington " on the Sussex Downs

60   The old Lock-up at Lingfield, Surrey

61 The Surrey Downs near Reigate

north it is protected by the beeches, on the south the down turf sweeps up to the long white windows. This is the most beautiful house in Sussex, and its furniture is as beautiful as any in the world.

To-day it is the home of Admiral Meade-Featherstonehaugh —how he came to inherit the house makes a very curious and complete story. It starts in the middle of the eighteenth century, when a buck of the Regency was born here, Sir Harry Featherstone Haugh. He came to be a great personal friend of the Prince Regent; together they enjoyed drinking-bouts in the Gothic Revival "Folly" built on the down to commemorate Sir Harry's coming-of-age; or there were orgies in the house, when Lady Hamilton would dance on the dining-room table—Sir Harry was Emma's first protector. This table, which is still in the house, was later to play a part in the life of another notable woman—as we shall see. That the rake should find himself unpopular with his neighbours of West Sussex was natural; for no stiffer county society exists, and he became no more respected when he decided to marry and settle down at the age of seventy-three—the county still refused to call, for he chose for his bride a Miss Bullock, a young dairymaid from one of his farms. Immediately after the wedding he sent her to France to be educated as a lady—and a thorough education it must have been; she did not return until her husband was approaching eighty. As the couple drove up to the house a girl of twelve, who was standing at the gate, curtsied and threw a nosegay. Sir Harry stopped the carriage, to find that the child was his sister-in-law; he made her get in and drive up to the house. She, too, was packed off to France to become a lady, after which, for the next ten years, the old rake and the two sisters lived quite alone; probably these were the happiest —certainly the most comfortable—years of his life. He died in 1840 at the age of ninety-two.

He had no heirs. Up Park went to his wife, and on her death, some years later, to her sister, who took the name of Miss Featherstone Haugh. This superb house and its furniture thus became the property of a peasant girl who—in spite of her unexpected French education—still spoke in a strong Sussex dialect. They were left to her completely in her gift; she might have sold what she wished, gone out into the world, travelled, or at least settled in some other neighbourhood and found real friends. Her travelling consisted of a stately afternoon drive through the lanes of Harting in a carriage and four —she had no desire to travel farther; for her only thought was to preserve the trust her sister had passed on. She lived

K

on here in state and alone until her death. A charming thought : this village girl, brought up in a cottage, to start life, no doubt, as a second housemaid, now mending and cleaning her own priceless damasks and Spitalfields silks. It is, in fact, owing to her humble origin that the furniture, curtains, chair covers and carpets of Up Park are unique—as spick and span as when first purchased over two hundred years ago ; and to her housekeeper and friend who helped her, our second notable woman who polished the table-top on which Emma Hamilton had danced ; she was the mother of H. G. Wells.

In her old age the mistress of the house had still one thought : that on her death the furniture should be cared for, and her adopted name preserved. For her heirs she chose two great friends whom she could trust : first, a Colonel Keith Turnour, and, in succession, Admiral Meade. Both were selected as second sons who could, therefore, adopt her name. She chose well ; when I called I found the Admiral digging in the garden ; in the drawing-room his wife was mending a pair of embroidered curtains with a devotion that would have satisfied the homely old peasant woman—Miss Featherstone Haugh.

VII

BEAUTY SPOTS

I

A TRAVELLER approaching the border of Surrey, between Rogate and Haslemere, receives a warning of what is to come : Rogate Common—a sandy plateau of bracken, heather, conifers and silver birch. For at this point the county overlaps its boundary. Elsewhere the opposite is the case : the southern border between Cranleigh and Lingfield might well be Sussex; the eastern, at Westerham, is more of Kent. Surrey has, in fact, been compared to an embroidered tablecloth, plain in the centre and pretty round the border ; which was another way of saying that she borrows her beauty from her neighbours. That is largely true.

Friends had warned me : " You'll have a job finding much to write about Surrey." They were right. (But I must here admit prejudice. Having passed the least pleasant years of my life in the Camberley district—private school, public school, and the Royal Military College—I suffer from an acute coniferphobia which it would be unfair to expect my reader to share). Others remarked : " Anyhow you can at least be funny about it." But they were wrong ; for I feel more sorry for this countryside which is cursed—cursed by a sandy soil that cherishes larches, wellingtonia and rhododendrons, and makes such excellent ground for manœuvring tanks and troops ; and cursed by Sir George Gilbert Scott, who has left in his home county only a handful of ancient churches not completely rebuilt (even early " Victorian Gothic " has not escaped) ; and, above all, cursed by its " Beauty Spots," close enough to London to entice week-enders many years before the motor-car came into popular use. During the summer months " well appointed " horse coaches used to leave the Victoria and Metropole hotels in London, and " drive through the most beautiful parts of the county."

Realising this, we can understand the peculiar despoliation of Surrey—more particularly Western Surrey—which is quite different to what is going on in Sussex and Kent to-day. Promiscuous building started much earlier in a comparatively small way, and has latterly been checked by the National Trust. Discounting the suburbs of London, quite a large proportion of Surrey is waste land. Though grateful to those benefactors who have, to some extent, forestalled a bungalow growth, one wonders whether the cure has not proved as painful as the disease. For the landscape itself has been violated; official car parks, benches, and litter baskets urbanise every lake and prominent hill; not a cottage fails to proclaim that wayside menace : " Minerals."

There is beauty still to be found—a beauty now only seen in the winter dusk, or from a railway train, that so often provides an unexpected " behind the scenes " view. I was travelling one spring afternoon down to Horsham and dozed off as the train left Victoria. I woke to find framed in the window a most lovely landscape of grass fields and a sauntering river, sheltered under steep wooded hills. I must have slept long past Horsham, for this valley was surely somewhere in Wiltshire or Devon. The name of a station flashed past; I had barely left the suburbs of London. We were running through the valley between Norbury Park and Box Hill.

For the purpose of this book I returned later by car. I selected a secondary road that branches off the Dorking-Reigate concrete road and passes over the highest crest of Box Hill, to Burford Bridge. On the map it looked most promising : a series of hairpin bends ; more promising was a warning that the slope was 1 in 5, and that motorists proceeded at their own risk. Having taken the risk and reached the summit, my sentiments were those of a mountaineer who has conquered a dangerous peak to discover a funicular railway disgorging tourists on the other side. I found a tarmac road bordered by camping-sites and bathing-pools. There were benches at every view-point, wire baskets for litter, and a heavy fall of litter on the threadbare turf.

Norbury Park across the valley was saved by Lord Beaverbrook, and is further protected by being closed to motor traffic. Only an occasional bus ticket, and the level drone of by-pass traffic, bring an urban note to this dark walk under Druids' yews. The yews conquer, shutting out all life and the sun. Through a gap, where a decrepit tree had fallen, I could see a curve of the new " Dual Carriage Way " that follows the old Roman road. From this distance, the traffic seemed to

62 The Devil's Punch Bowl from the Surrey Heaths, near Hindhead

63   A Surrey Hay Field

64 Almshouses by Gilbert Scott at Godstone, Surrey

65 The Aftermath of Trippers, Box Hill, Surrey

66   Restoration Brickwork at Godalming, Surrey

67   Norman Church Interior at Compton, Surrey

move as slowly as the orderly double procession to and from a nest of ants. The sun shone with the precision of the electric beam that discloses life on the microscope slide.

II

That romantic range of sea shells, the North Downs, reaches a crescendo and grand finale at Box Hill. As far as Kent, Sussex, and Surrey are concerned, the performance is over. Then there is an accidental kick of the drum !—the Hog's Back, a razor-edged ridge that peters out above Farnham. It is the poorest of Surrey's accredited beauty spots ; but though the landscape may be mediocre, the traveller's comforts reach a climax. On this last westerly spur stands the " Hog's Back Hotel " : BRASSERIE, GRILL ROOM, RESTAURANT, COCKTAIL BAR, ITALIAN GARDEN, TOWER LOUNGE—the most unexpected luxury hotel in the whole countryside. Looking north and south from the Tower Lounge, the visitor " enjoys " two panoramic views. In appearance they are somewhat similar ; in character these two tracts of country are unrelated, for the Hog's Back is an important dividing line. North of this line is no place for tourists—the sandy soil belongs almost exclusively to the Military, Racing Motorists, and the Dead.

Pirbright, Bisley, Bagshot, Camberley—to how many Englishmen must these names bring gruesome memories of military training, from flagging O.T.C. field-days to staff college rides !

At Brooklands is the world's first motor-racing track. It was laid down in 1906, with banking for cars travelling at a hundred miles per hour—at that time the maximum speed ever hoped for. To-day, the result of a race depends, not so much on the speed of the car, as on the motorist who can drive the fastest without going over the top.

Outside Woking is England's largest cemetery, " The London Necropolis," covering some four miles of " wild, undulating, healthy land." It was laid out and planted with wellingtonia by a private company in 1852. To-day the cemetery has its own " Necropolis station "—the engine drivers are reputed to wear top-hats, black gloves and crêpe. This forest of headstones and wellingtonia—which is only comparable to Scutari's forest of cypresses and Mohammedan tombs—will present an astonishing landscape when the trees reach their full height of six hundred feet.

Should the reader wish to explore further this north-west corner of Surrey, he must do so on his own. I could find

L

nothing of interest, nothing of beauty, except, one dark sodden afternoon, a line of tanks rolling and pitching over the crest of Chobham Common ; a beauty that was *macabre*.

South of the Hog's Back ridge the landscape is reserved for tourists; here we find the remainder of Surrey's Beauty Spots : Frensham Ponds, The Devil's Punch Bowl, Gibbet Hill, The Silent Pool, and, farther east, Leith and Pitch Hills.

The 108-acre sheet of water south of Frensham is less a beauty spot than a pleasure resort : in the summer, little sailing boats tack backward and forward like toy boats on the " Round Pond " ; on shore picnickers' buttocks have worn away all grass, leaving a fine bathing beach of sand.

The church at Frensham provides a tourist's trophy : a huge witch's cauldron—three feet across—in which a certain Mother Ludlam is said to have boiled her " eye of newt and toe of frog, wool of bat and tongue of dog, adder's fork and blindworm's sting, lizard's leg and howlet's wing," and any other ingredients necessary for the working of her spells. The parish priest, so the story goes, stole her cauldron, washed it out with holy water and placed it in the church. In fact, these vessels were once to be found in almost every parish and were used for mulling beer at local feasts.

At Hindhead, three miles to the south, the scenery is spectacular ; the Devil's Punch Bowl is well named—except that those who invented the Devil had not yet invented punch. But the interest of this landscape is geological rather than historical : " The whole tract . . . is wild and barren in its aspect, destitute of wood, and producing only ferns, heaths, and furze. The surface is, in fact, to this hour, nearly such as it may be conceived to have been when first un-covered by the sea " (Fitton). Shut your ears to the motor traffic, and eyes to the Christmas trees : you have England as it must have appeared to the first man.

The valley of the bowl is, I believe, a hunting ground for the botanist—in particular, collectors of ferns. The following wild plants were noted by Murray (1897) and J. C. Cox, LL.D., F.S.A. (1910) : The flowering fern, the sweet mountain fern, and the marsh fern ; the bog pimpernel, drosera, the guelder rose, three varieties of bladder heath, three of milkwort, two of potentilla, cow-wheat, sneeze-wort, and the lesser skull-cap. But whether any roots have been left, I am too ignorant of botany to say.

Above the bowl, south of the Portsmouth road, stands Gibbet Hill, popular both for its " extensive views over the Weald " and gruesome memories of three murderers who

68   Derby Day at Epsom

69   The View from Gibbet Hill, Hindhead, Surrey

70   Frensham Great Pond, in the " Surrey Highlands "

71   The Village Pump, Newdigate, Surrey

72   The Churchyard, Newdigate, Surrey

hung here in chains on a gibbet in 1786. Their memory
has been kept green by a James Sitwell of Cosford, who
erected a stone " in detestation of a barbarous murder com-
mitted here on an unknown sailor. . . ." The murdered man
was on his way to rejoin his ship. He fell in with three other
sailors and, being flush, generously offered to treat them as
far as Portsmouth. Later, his naked body was discovered
lying halfway down the slope of the Punch Bowl, and that
same evening his three murderers were arrested at Rake while
attempting to sell the victim's clothes. How little can he
have foreseen — this man without even a name — that his
memory would be drawing a crowd two hundred years later.

Sitwell seems to have had all the dictatorial, but endearing,
characteristics of the eighteenth-century squire ; on the back
of the monument he inscribed, " Cursed be the man who
injureth or removeth this stone." The inscription has gone,
but all attempts have failed to remove this relic considered
so unsuited to a Surrey beauty spot. In the end, the best
that could be done was to put up a rival monument in better
taste : a most unexpected Celtic cross was placed on the hilltop by Sir William Erle in 1851. At the same time his brother
presented a direction dial. To-day the summit of the hill is
without a blade of grass.

Leith Hill, too, has its bald patch. That is only natural,
for it is the highest point in the Weald, and I think I am right
in saying that there is no higher hill in the three counties
covered by this book. I seem to remember, from school,
that 1000 feet justified the title of " mountain." Under this
classification Leith Hill can just claim the distinction if we
include the watch tower on the summit. In any case the flat
roof of this Folly provides many long-distance records to be
won : thirteen counties ; forty-one London churches and
Big Ben ; the chapel of Lancing College ; Dungeness ;
and " On 15th July 1844, the air being remarkably clear, a
party of the Ordnance Surveyors then encamped on the hill,
saw with the naked eye an observatory, only 9 ft. square,
near Ashford, in Kent ; and with a small telescope, a staff
only 4 in. in diameter, on Dunstable Downs " (Brayley).

The tower was built by an eighteenth-century farmer,
Richard Hull, to serve as his own burial-place and a benefit
to all comers. On a wall-tablet, since destroyed, he described
himself as a man intimate with Pope, Trenchard, and Bishop
Berkeley, and " a true Christian and rural philosopher."
But—as in the case of almost every Folly—a foolish legend
has been evolved : " The hill is crowned by a small structure,

traditionally said to mark the spot where an eccentric farmer of the neighbourhood was buried on horseback upside down, so that, when the world was turned, as he believed it then soon would be, topsy-turvy, he might at last come up in the right position " (Topographical Dictionary of England and Wales).

One wonders what stories will be told of Lord Berners in a hundred years' time.[1]

The subsequent history of Hull's Tower is an indication of the wild state of Leith Hill and the surrounding country at the beginning of the last century; instead of chocolate-munching toponymists, only smugglers and thieves made use of the building, and, a few years after Hull's death, a subscription had to be raised among the local gentry for bricking and cementing up the windows and doors. This was so efficiently carried out that it was impossible to reopen the tower in more peaceful times, and an outer staircase to the roof was added in 1859.

Farther to the west, Pitch Hill and Hurt Wood retained their wild aspect until a few years ago. This heath was known only to enthusiastic ramblers and the gipsies who encamped here throughout the year. To-day the gipsies have been moved on (perhaps a time will come when they will be put back and forbidden to leave by the National Trust), and the ramblers have developed into hikers; but these five miles between Holmbury St. Mary and Shamley Green are still the least sophisticated stretch of Wealden Surrey.

There remains " The Silent Pool " and the neighbouring village of Shere. The village is pretty enough but incomparable to Betchworth, for instance, which never is—and I pray never will be—visited at all. In " The Silent Pool " I found a beauty which neither MINERALS nor POSTCARDS—not even Tennyson's "netted sunbeam"—could make banal. Yet, of all Surrey's beauty spots this is the one that provoked the late Rev. Charles Cox to use strong language for a Surrey rambler: " . . . To my mind its beauty and gloom have been much exaggerated, and associated with crazy romance as set forth in Martin Tupper's foolish book, *Stephen Langton*. The whole of the present associations of this place strike me as eminently artificial."

So perhaps it is perversity that leads me to select this sombre indigo pool as a " Beauty Spot " that has beauty. Perhaps it is because I have only seen it once in dim autumn twilight under dripping trees.

[1] Lord Berners' " Folly " tower at Faringdon was recently designed by Lord G. Wellesley.

73 Betchworth, Surrey : Old Cottages

74 Betchworth, Surrey : Georgian Façade

75　Chiddingly Place, Sussex—now inhabited by tinkers

76　Stacking Hay on the South Downs

CHAPTER

VIII

THE ROAD TO THE COAST

I

ON my way to Lewes I can make a detour through lanes that take me to Chiddingly. The spire of the church can be seen from the Eastbourne road, but few motorists turn off, though its shape might well attract them ; for it is a broach spire of very great beauty, and beneath it stands one of the most charming small churches to be found in Sussex. In the churchyard yews frame the thin-washed line of the South Downs. Inside the church, Early English arches of grey stone frame the alabaster tomb of Sir John Jefferay, Lord Chief Baron of the Exchequer. The composition is striking : in the centre recline two figures, Sir John and his first wife, Alice, flanked on each side by the standing figures of Dame Elizabeth, their heiress daughter, and her husband, Baron Edward Montagu of Boughton. In the centre kneels their child.

Dame Elizabeth's appearance is stupendous ; her hair is woven a foot high in the form of a fan, and bound with strings of amber—it is as fantastic as the glue-set carved coiffure of a Shilluk warrior. From the ruff a collar rises like a peacock's tail. The tight stomacher, above which the naked breasts protrude, is as straight and as narrow as a stove pipe. From the hips hangs " the bawd farthingale " in voluminous brocaded folds.

The monument is obscured by a row of spiked railings. During the Reformation the figures were badly mutilated, but these railings are now mere examples of " shutting the stable door," and should be removed.

65   M

On the north wall of the chancel is a small monument to Margaret, wife of Thomas Jeffrey, who is shown with her two daughters ; of the mother is written :

> Flesh is but flesh
> The farest flowers do fall
> The strongest Stoope
> Death is the end of all.

This carving also suffered during the Reformation, when the figures of the two daughters were decapitated. The heads have since been replaced in plaster by some local craftsman, giving these sisters an expression of fiendish jocularity which completely belies the four alliterated virtues with which they are attributed : " Prudens, Pie, Pulchra, Pudia."

About half a mile outside the village, on the Laughton road, there is one of the rarest curiosities in Sussex : Chiddingly Place, a red-brick manor house of great age and beauty. Darkened by yew trees, it stands alone in the fields —a sad romantic ruin. Once it was the seat of the Jefferays, a family so proud that when they walked from the manor to the church, the road, it is said, had to be paved with cheeses —a legend probably inspired by the monument we have just seen, in which Dame Elizabeth's foot is resting on a cushion shaped like a flat round cheese. Part of the front of the house has been refaced ; but the stained plaster is as derelict as the stone mullioned windows it frames. Over the doorway has been added a fanlight and an eighteenth-century portico, exquisitely carved.

The rest of the manor stands apart—two lofty wings of pale Elizabethan brick. Between the buildings fragments of old wall rise erratically out of the field.

Such is Chiddingly Place as it is to-day, and you may wonder why I find this ruin so curious ? The strange thing is that this great manor should be occupied—but not, as one might suppose, by gentry from London, or a local architect with taste. Like the Baroque Villa Palagonia outside Palermo, Chiddingly Place is now lived in by a family of tinkers—a very large family, Mr. and Mrs. Page, and too many children to count. There is also a black mongrel that does tricks, and, among the ruins and lines of washing, a tethered goat. Mr. Page " does bits of repairing to farm implements—when a job comes along." For " a carper " his fourteen-year-old son will show the sightseer " some sacred things " : a dungeon and an underground tunnel which (though it runs in the opposite direction for no more than a hundred yards) is

77 The Road to Lewes

78   Glyndebourne Opera-house

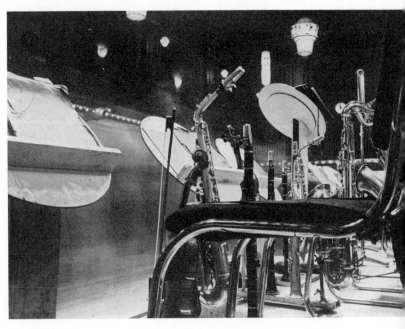

79   Sherry's at Brighton
The Interval

claimed by the boy to be a smuggler's secret passage ending in the church.

On my raising the "carper" to a "tanner," he took me with reluctance into the house. An old painted wallpaper hung in tatters over the staircase. I would have liked to explore further, but Mrs. Page reminded me that it was the dinner hour. I left them to their tea, margarine and bread.

II

Most Sussex guide-books warn the traveller to prepare for a shock at Glynde. Here is a church that is not in keeping; is not, as E. V. Lucas puts it, " the indigenous Sussex House of God "—in fact, a Renaissance church : a charming little building, shaded by cedar trees, built on the plan of a Greek temple in pale grey Sussex flints. Alas ! everything has been done to put things right : a Tudoresque lych-gate has been added, and the original clear glass has been replaced by some memorial stained glass of the 'nineties.

In the village are two famous Elizabethan houses : Glynde Place and Glyndebourne. The Place and its lovely stable gateway adjoin the church and are built of the same material ; as a group, these three buildings must be the largest and most handsome example of flintwork in England.

What name could be more suggestive than Glyndebourne of a secluded stream—a little Sussex valley where the same family has lived for eight hundred years ? And so it has been until five years ago, when the present descendant of this family, John Christie, attempted an experiment ; he staged a musical festival in his garden to compete with Salzburg and Bayreuth. The underlying principle of this experiment was to have full rehearsals, and a cast of uniform excellence instead of the mediocre singers outshone by a single famous star to be found in state-controlled opera. His was a war, in fact, against mediocrity ; and he claims that on " that first glamorous night of 1934," he put on an opening perform-ance of a standard never seen before. To-day, although the auditorium holds only six hundred, he has a stage larger than the Metropolitan Opera House in New York ; and employs over a hundred singers and musicians, and one of the finest living conductors in Herr Fritz Busch. Special trains run daily from London—evening-dressed figures crowd Victoria platform in the inappropriate light of the afternoon—and Glyndebourne is now featured in Travel

Agents' Brochures all over Europe and the United States. For the season only—then again it becomes a secluded Sussex home. But even the glory of the flowers has been confined to these few weeks. At the end of July, Mr. and Mrs. Christie must go to their other home in Cornwall ; for their Sussex garden is a garden gone to seed.

III

Lewes Castle was built by a Norman earl, William de Warrenne, son-in-law of William the Conqueror. The architect's plan was unusual, with two separate keeps—they are all that remain standing to-day ; the rest is a ruin transformed into sheltered terraces of gardens and lawn. The few rooms open to the public serve as a museum, but, above all, this is a place just to sit and read on a summer's afternoon, or—by climbing many steep flights of circling stairs on to the leads of the tower—to look down on other people's houses, examine their roofs for leakages, and share their contentment in each thin column of smoke. It is indeed a peaceful if crazy perspective of Sussex tiles : in the centre, deep sepia weathered in patches of gamboge and ash grey, but becoming newer and redder as they radiate to the pink geranium bungalow roofs that strive to find some footing on the slopes of the Downs. In the east they have been arrested by the wall of " Cliffe Hill " ; in the south by the dykes of the Ouse. But northward they have filtered through the Lewes gap, and to the west they are not far now from the racecourse—and before long may smother the rough, gorse-covered hill beyond which is called " Mount Harry." Then, yet another landmark in history will have vanished, and with it the memory of the most murderous, bloody battle fought on Sussex soil.

This particular " Harry " was Henry III., who with his son Edward, and Richard, King of the Romans, was routed by Simon De Montfort in 1264. As in every Civil War, this " Battle of the Barons " was fought with a bitterness unknown between professional soldiers ; the day's casualties were six to eight thousand, and—as far as the Royal forces were concerned—all tactical considerations were scrapped out of lust to kill.

De Montfort and his Barons had encamped eight miles to the north at Fletching. The Bishops of London and Worcester who had accompanied him, hoping to negotiate with the King, sang masses throughout the night. The great nave of Fletching Church had been completed only a few years; but it has changed little during the centuries, and one can still visualise the steady flames of candles and unwieldy figures filing up to the altar — lowering themselves cautiously in clanky armour to pass the night in prayer.

At dawn De Montfort led his army in file through the Weald (it was May, and one wonders how shrill the bird chorus in so dense a forest must have been); and then out into the spring sunlight of the bare down. Here he deployed into four divisions, placing one on each of those three spurs that run past the racecourse into the town, and the fourth in reserve on the " Mount."

King Henry also spent the eve of the battle on holy ground —in the Priory of St. Pancras. But, for his troops, it was a night of bragging and debauchery, carried on even in the great choir of the church. There could be no cause for prayer; the morrow's battle must have seemed just a good day's sport—particularly to Prince Edward; hardly had the " Royal Dragon " been properly unfurled, and his father got off his famous challenge " Simon je vous defye," than the young prince was out of sight, leading a dashing cavalry charge on De Montfort's left wing.

Before the invention of the cross-bow, a charge of heavy cavalry, with both horse and warrior completely armoured, must have been as destructive against infantry in the open as the first tanks: De Montfort's citizen army dropped their pikes and longbows, and scattered and ran. But—with the intuition of the hunted—they soon discovered that they could outstrip these great cumbersome carthorses by bolting straight up, and again straight down the steepest sides of the hills. This chivvying went on for the better part of the day; and then the Prince found a further diversion in a closed litter, left prominently on a hill, and marked by De Montfort's pennons and standard. This he attacked with such zest that it was not until too late that he discovered he had been hoaxed into killing some Royal hostages bound and gagged inside. It was late afternoon when he trotted—self-satisfied in spite of his last *gaffe*—back on to the scene of battle; he should be nicely in time to turn his father's victory into a slaughter —nicely in time for another hour or two's sport. But the battle on the Downs was over; De Montfort had thrown the whole of his reserve division against the weakened Royalist army, routed it, and forced the King of England to take shelter in the Priory of St. Pancras and the King of the Romans in a windmill that then stood in the town. With difficulty did the Prince fight his way through the streets to join his father behind the massive Priory walls.

Outside these walls the battle continued with savage chaos —" eyther desyrous to bring the other out of lyfe." By nightfall many houses were fired, and in their leaping glare massed troops would clash unexpectedly at street corners, while solitary frightened men scurried hither and thither, up and down the steep, narrow alleys. And the noise must have been terrific when—above all the bashing and shouting and screaming—the death of one knight sounded like an avalanche of tiles.

But all this confused terror of battle was nothing compared to the final flight. Those of Prince Edward's knights who had been shut out of the Priory attempted to retire across the river Ouse to the Castle of Pevensey. As always in battle, such news passed with the swiftness of radio telegraphy to every rank—" We're lost . . . RETREAT . . . RETREAT ! "

There was but one bridge across the river—probably a narrow wooden bridge, carried for some distance on piles so as to cross both the river and the deep marshes on either side. Of the hundreds jostled over the edge, the foot-soldiers sank in the mud out of sight ; but the knights on their great armoured carthorses were discovered next morning, for each of their lances still showed, like a submarine's periscope, above the surface ; they sat, firmly strapped to their saddles, holding up these lances in lifeless hands.

Looking down on this homely market town, or across the pink geranium bungalow roofs to the gaunt grand-stand on the race-course, it is difficult indeed to visualise this bloody battle of Lewes. The marshes have been drained for meadows ; the King of the Romans' windmill has been replaced by the Black Horse Inn ; the Castle, as we have seen, is a pleasure garden where—in preference to a hotel bedroom—one comes to pass a sleepy summer hour ; and the great Priory of St. Pancras —that, too, has achieved some sort of peace as a Sports Club.

The Priory was founded by the same Earl de Warrenne who built Lewes Castle—and his wife Gundrada. The building has practically disappeared. When Cromwell decided to destroy it he sent an expert ; in a letter to his master this agent describes how the place was " hewn, cut away, plucked down, and pulled to the ground." To-day it is difficult to imagine the original building except its size ; it covered forty acres ; and everywhere, between the bowling-greens, putting-courses, and tennis-courts, appear fragments of ivied masonry :

80   Lewes Junction and the Downs

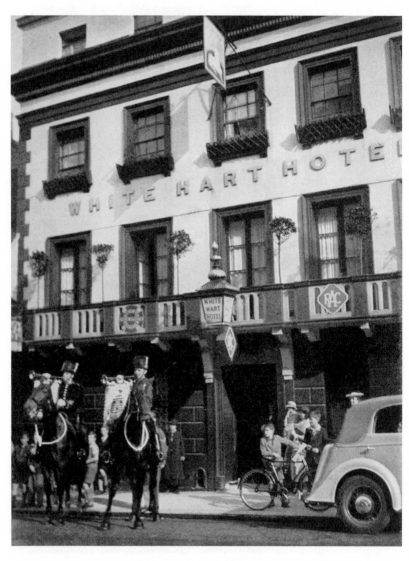

81   The " White Hart " at Lewes

a stone altar, short stretches of wall, or a portion of an arch which rise from these green lawns like rocks out of the sea. At the northern boundary stands " The Mount," a conical hill surmounted by a flagpole and cut into by one of the bowling-greens. Some say this was a calvary—for a penance monks had to carry earth to the summit from a sunken field now known as " The Dripping Pan." It is as a calvary that it is marked on the Ordnance map. Other authorities claim that the mound was the site of William Warrenne's first castle; there are others who compare it to salt pans on the Essex coast. We must leave " The Mount " as being a conical feature of the landscape, and an enjoyable bone for archæologists to pick.

Within these forty acres is Southover Church—it stands on the Lewes–Newhaven road. Both exterior and interior are depressing, but in a modern side chapel built by public subscription in unpleasant Caen stone lie the bodies of de Warrenne and his wife, Gundrada. That husband and wife should be both resting once more together, *and* beneath their original tombstone, approaches a miracle. Only the thrift of a Sir Thomas Shurley saved the tomb from Cromwell's destruction : seeing the Priory being demolished, he carted off the slab to help build his own monument in Isfield Church, seven miles away. Towards the end of the eighteenth century it was retrieved by the antiquarian, Sir William Burrell, and placed as an exhibit in Southover Church. The second part of the miracle occurred over half a century later, when the bodies of the two founders were discovered by labourers of the London, Brighton and South Coast Railway, who were cutting their first line through the Priory grounds. The remains were in two leaden caskets, marked simply " Willhelm " and " Gundrada." The empty caskets now stand in niches of the chapel wall ; the bones rest under the ancient stone in the centre of the floor. The slab bears an inscription in Latin which, freely translated, reads :

" *Gundrada of ruling stock, the glory of her age, brought into the churches a noble offspring of the balsam of English ways.*
Martir . . . (portion broken)
To the wretched she was Martha ; of her piety she was Mary. Dead is the part of Martha ; Mary, the greater part, survives.
O pious Pancras, that testifies to piety and justice, she makes thee her heir ; do thou, gentle one, take on thyself the mother's part.
The sixth day of the Kalends of June came upon her and broke the alabaster shell of her flesh."

IV

There are many peculiarities about Brighton—too many to enumerate in full. But how strange it is, for instance, that a town built on a series of precipitous hills should have escaped the title of " England's Rome " ; escaped only because nine hundred and ninety-nine visitors out of every thousand have always thought the rest of this vast town as flat as the promenade. Another peculiarity is Brighton's weather : perpetual sunshine is the verdict of most visitors, but here again they are referring to the promenade and not the town. I have stood for hours on one of the back hills and watched clouds materialise before my eyes. They appear from nowhere, forming a solid layer, and the edge of this layer seems quite motionless in spite of a strong sea breeze ; for as each cloud is blown inland another is formed to take its place. Beyond, to the south, the sky is clear down to the horizon, and the sea viridian specked with flashes of sunlit waves : the two piers and the pleasure steamer are startling white ; figures stroll basking on the promenade. And all the time the servants' bedrooms at the back of the great hotels are in depressing shadow and the streets are damp with a drizzle of rain.

But I find most curious about this town the fact that—in spite of all the wailings of successive generations—its character has so little changed. The old type of life may become fuller : new types are added ; but the two have rarely merged. The fishermen of the little village of Brighthelmstone must have seemed doomed to extinction when, in 1750, Dr. Russell of Lewes popularised the curative powers of sea-bathing and sea-air—but the fishing trade of Brighton flourishes as ever. Next the town became the playground of royalty and " bucks," and their frivolity might well have banished all invalids—but bath-chairs and sun shelters are as popular to-day. And much the same applies to the buildings and entertainments : Wells Coates' fine block of luxury flats has not yet (thank Heaven) inspired Mr. Pitt of the " Cricketers' Arms." Nor have the new cinemas affected the " peep-shows " on the piers : " What Tommy saw in Paris " is as heavily clothed as forty years ago.

The logical result of all this is that the town's patrons also remain in clear-cut compartments—so isolated that they are unconscious of each other's existence. The phrase " I'm

82   The Sea Front at Hove : Regency and Twentieth Century

83   Brighton Crooner

running down to Brighton for the week-end " is thrown out
as casually by race gangsters, collectors of old musical boxes,
hypochondriacs, curb crawlers in sports cars, patient pier-end
fishermen or night-club queens—and always with the assumption that everyone visits Brighton for no other reason than
their own.

But there is one object in the town over which visitors
meet on common ground—though admittedly the ground
may be one of disagreement : the Royal Pavilion cannot be
ignored.   Whoever passes—gangster, fisherman, hypochondriac, or collector of antiques—he must pause to express
either pleasure or disgust.   Which they will express is beyond
conjecture, and any reader who likes a lead in matters of taste
can be assured that this is a case when he can say what he
thinks without fear.   For there are four main categories into
which public opinion can be roughly divided : amongst
the lowest of all brows—" the proletariat "—this ornate
travesty of the east calls for their genuine admiration, particularly when flood-lit purple, green and red ; on the other
hand, the normal brow—" the man in the street "—considers
it in the worst possible taste.   Among the highbrows it has
long been understood that the building was divine—and to
have disagreed would have been to class oneself a " Blimp."
But within the last year or two a most disconcerting figure
has arisen : a new super kingpin of the highest brow who—
without even fair warning—refers to the Royal Pavilion as
" too ghastly for words."

N

IX

THE COAST ROAD TO THE WEST

I

THE coast road west from Brighton is now linked to Shoreham by seven miles of stucco-and-brick cottages— but by nothing else. There is, and always will be, a fundamental difference between these two towns. It is the difference between a sea that is bathed in and a sea that is sailed by ships. You notice the change as soon as you reach Portslade : instead of piers and promenades and fun fairs, you find cranes and high smoking chimneys ; timber yards, coal stacks, petroleum tanks, grimy brick ware-houses, black tarred wharfs, the sound of riveting, and the smell of gas.

Shoreham has now become two villages since the retreat of the sea—New and Old Shoreham—and they both have churches of the greatest interest. Of the church at New Shoreham only the chancel, the tower, and two short aisles remain. When the Adur became silted up in the fifteenth century, the port had to be abandoned and the town became half deserted. There was no longer need for so large a church, and in any case no funds to support it, so the nave was used as a quarry, and has now completely disappeared. Previously to this, Old Shoreham had been left stranded in the same way : in the twelfth century it was the main port between England and Normandy ; it now hides in shame a mile to the north —an isolated hamlet of farm buildings, thatched cottages, and a church of richly carved Norman arches—all penned in on one side by an aerodrome and on the other by a new concrete road. Between the two villages are the Swiss gardens, once

84   The Palace Pier, Brighton

85 "The Cricketers' Hotel," Brighton

the equivalent of London's Vauxhall Gardens. History moves fast in Sussex; this playground of the 'eighties is already billed as "Ye Olde Swiss Gardens"—and customs change; the jazz band plays *only* on Sundays.

II

No sooner do you leave Shoreham than Worthing comes to meet you. Along the coast road these two towns are linked by bungalows set among "Lidos" and "Golden Beaches"—bungalows of every period of architecture in history erected during the last twenty years. But this can be avoided by paying a toll of sixpence at the Old Shoreham wooden bridge and taking the inland road. Do this and see Sompting Church. According to *Murray's Handbook* a field path leads to the church, which stands in a grove of elms, and the key should be inquired for at the vicarage. To-day there is a road to the church door, which is unlocked, and most of the elms have been lopped. Otherwise this very odd building must look much as it did eight hundred years ago—of Saxon origin, the surprising tower might have been the model for the modern Swedish school of ecclesiastical architecture; and the interior of the church is as original in plan: the main porch is in the southern transept, from which a flight of steps lead up to the level of the nave, but there are no steps to the altar; the north transept is subdivided into two by three Early English arches; and the font is in a minute recessed chapel which once had its own altar.

Ten years ago there stood in the marshes between Sompting and Worthing the village of West Tarring with its Early English church and street of seventeenth-century half-timbered cottages. Now it has been engulfed by Worthing's detached "Ideal Homes" at £699 down, and to-day the church is difficult enough to find in spite of its spire, which is so lofty that it served as a watch-tower during the threat of the Spanish Armada. It is impossible to find the street of half-timbered cottages because all but one have been pulled down. This one has been preserved by the Sussex Architectural Society and is now open to the public. Among the ideal homes is an orchard of fig trees; some authorities claim that the trees were planted by Thomas à Becket (Tarring was one of his favourite peculiars); others give the credit to St. Richard de la Wich of Chichester. No matter—to this day the fig trees have survived all new housing schemes. They still bear fruit.

III

Having reached Worthing by one route or the other, we soon leave it. Not that there is anything to be said against the town, but there is nothing particular to be mentioned in its favour. Like Brighton, Worthing is purely a pleasure resort; like Brighton, it was first popularised by the Guelphs —Princess Amelia in 1799. But Nash did not follow her; except for two or three Regency buildings every lodging-house in Worthing looks like a lodging-house. The promenade is three miles long.

From now on, until we have passed Bognor, there is little respite; only here and there are to be found small isolated reminders of the days when this coast was productive farmland—the English must be the only people in the world prepared to pay fifty times more for the land they live on than for the land that provides them with food; imagine speculative building in the vineyards of Medoc or Hungary's plains of wheat. Here the transformation has been sudden: in Ferring I met a publican who had witnessed the change and regretted the days when his only clients were labourers who walked three miles for their evening beer. With three thousand new inhabitants one would have thought that his business would have improved. "But they're only here a month in the year, sir," he complained—"then they bring their own stores."

While trying to find your way through this villa-growth, Ferring, Angmering-on-Sea and Goring (which is difficult enough, as most avenues are dead ends), you discover little patches of beauty which in this setting seem divine: a shower of white lilac; a sterile creeper still clutching an old wall; a plough lying rusty against the trunk of an elm.

At Goring-on-Sea there is a skyline that might be the seashore of Livorno, the indigo skyline of umbrella pines —here the trees are huge ilex, that stretch in an avenue a mile long. To-day this avenue is as inexplicable as unexpected: imprisoned by unfinished villas, it leads from nothing to nowhere. There is easy access from the various concrete roads and paths which happen to cut through it; but at each end are immense wrought-iron gates kept locked.

Within a mile of Angmering there is a reminder of Sussex's

more ancient past, a Roman villa now in the process of excavation. It was winter—presumably not the " digging " season—when I visited the site ; over five acres, stretched water-logged trenches and rectangular patches of foundation —black tarpaulins kept down with stones covered the more important finds ; I lifted a corner to see black insects scurrying over a square yard of tiles. I looked through the window of a little wooden shack and saw shelves of oddments—everything precisely labelled, even down to " Large Empty Tins." Outside the shed, on a rickety table, lay a selection of tile and brick fragments, and oyster shells still offered for sale at a penny or twopence apiece. On a post was nailed a biscuit tin with a slit for contributions ; the rusty lid had warped open, showing a rainwater-filled void. On this winter evening these relics seemed more lost than during all their seventeen hundred years under Sussex soil.

IV

For years the genteel have referred to Littlehampton as " a nice quiet little place, my dear " ; for years the Corporation have banned all fun ; to-day that admirable firm, Butlins, have had their way ; their giant racer (which, though Reckitt's Blue, manages somehow to look like the Roman amphitheatre at Nîmes) has stolen whatever amusement value the little old wooden pier could offer. I found the same firm cheering up Bognor's promenade : Fun Fairs and plaster " Rockies " had shattered the façade of respectable lodginghouses, for ever reminiscing over the visit of the late King George V.

Among the suburbs of Bognor is to be found the thatched village of Felpham. William Blake lived here in " Felpham Cottage, of cottages the prettiest," and there is now a road named after him, and his home is preserved much as it was— though slightly arted up.

In the large castellated house lived his patron, William Hayley—rich man, shocking horseman (he always rode with an open umbrella and always fell off), and inferior poet. That such a relationship should end sadly was as inevitable then as it would be to-day ; sooner or later the genius must bite the feeding hand. A provocation for biting came when Blake was accused of treason. He had forcibly turned out a soldier from his garden, who, in revenge, accused the poet of having used seditious language against the King. The charge was probably without foundation, and—largely owing to Hayley's intervention—the case was dismissed. But the seed of grievance had been sown ; Blake was now a victim of conspiracy—such must have been the feelings of D. H. Lawrence when he was stupidly arrested in the war as a spy— all the world wished to persecute him, and the rich Hayley was, of course, the villain behind the scene. Blake left his garden, where " voices of celestial inhabitants are more distinctly heard, their forms more distinctly seen " ; where he had observed a fairy's funeral—the body laid on a rose leaf— and where he had conversed with angels who were seated in the trees.

V

Any traveller with normal curiosity would go out of his way to explore the dead end of Selsey—Seals Island, where Wilfrid of York was shipwrecked in A.D. 680, and took the opportunity to convert the Saxons away from their gods Woden, Odin and Thor. When he landed there had been no rain for three years ; he found near-skeletons that had chained themselves together, and were about to end their sufferings by walking into the sea. First he taught them how to fish with nets, then providential rains came with his first baptism. So Wilfrid became the Saint of all fishermen.

But it is not only its history that entices the traveller to Selsey; look at it on the half-inch " Bartholomew "—the small letters isolated in the green-tinted peninsula, the handful of houses, the coastguard station, and church standing among marshes on Sussex's most southern shore. But there is no other place that denies so flatly its appearance on the map as this first-rate shopping centre in red brick, with its modern church and Palace Hotel.

It was this same map curiosity that persuaded me to explore a further two miles to a point on the wide Pagham creek, where I saw marked another church. Away from all other buildings I found a little stucco box, set with a great Perpendicular window, and standing among several acres of ancient graves. This is all that is left of the original thirteenth-century church of Selsey—the chancel. The rest was pulled down to be built into the new church of the red-brick town.

But unlike the destruction of Reculver, this was not vandalism ; the church had to be transplanted because the old town of Selsey had been claimed by the sea. The tide was out, and I walked on the bed of the estuary between flotsam and

86 Greater Brighton

87   Downland Farming, Clayton, Sussex

dark jade-green weed.   Beyond lay shallow brackish water
where tern wheeled crying, then closed their wings to drop
like stones.   Hidden beneath the seaweed I found the debris
of many buildings : foundations laid here hundreds of years
ago, and piles of new machine-stamped bricks from a row of
cottages that had lately stood on the point several miles away.
Farther out, under the shallow water, are the Saxon walls of
St. Wilfrid's Cathedral.   When a winter's night is moaning
you can hear the tolling of the bells—at least, so say the sailors
who are buffeted close to Selsey Bill.

CHAPTER

X

THE COAST ROAD EAST

I

A GREAT coast road travels east from Brighton, cutting thoughtlessly through Rottingdean, to Newhaven. In its wake it has left a litter of unpleasant pleasure resorts. The village of Rottingdean—quaint, picturesque, the home of Kipling and Sir Edward Burne-Jones, and within only three miles of Brighton—can have never hoped to escape the estate agents' attention. Yet, in 1904, E. V. Lucas wrote : " The Little Village is hardly ever likely to creep over its surrounding hills. . . ." That was just about the time that I arrived for my first term at the Georgian-fronted private school that stands back from the main street. Whether the houses were old or new, pretty or hideous, was no concern of a boy of seven ; but I do remember the windy empty road as we drove from Brighton in a wagonette ; and I do remember that—according to the headmaster's daughter—a wild cat (a sheep-killer) lived just beyond the playing-fields on the bare down. Perhaps it was true ; the country was desolate enough —the little village had not yet started " to creep over its surrounding hills." How exasperating it must be to a lover of nature who still has his home in Rottingdean : as he grows more decrepit, so he must walk farther and farther to escape the Tudoresque tentacles that writhe out from the Tudor Close.

But there is another side to these downland villages ; to see that you must travel, beyond the tentacles, inland to Ballsdean. It is best to walk there. A journey by car should be made only under the following circumstances : there has been no rain for at least a week ; you have a passenger to open the gates ; your car inspires no pride of ownership.

88 The Desecration of the Downs : Saltdean, on the Coast Road to Brighton

89   The " Grid " crossing the Sussex Downs

90 The View from Bury Hill over the Sussex Downs

91 Lullington, in the Cuckmere Valley : a fragment

92 Westmeston, near Lewes, with the characteristic catslide roof

Typical Sussex Churches

There is nothing of great interest or beauty at Ballsdean except a fine red-brick Georgian farmhouse standing in its "dean" below a cold sweep of down; but the journey is worth while if only to look at this other picture; for here there is no fumed oak half-timbering; no arty-crafty shops. Almost all trace of the village has disappeared except for some ruined walls, dumps of scrap-iron, and a little Perpendicular chapel with a corrugated-iron roof, which is now used as a tool-shed. To emphasise the barrenness of the down, there roams a herd of Belted Galloways—a hardy breed of cattle from the Highlands—which, a farm-lad informed me, knew how to look after themselves.

According to the map, the track goes on to Kingston, but I advise returning the way you came, and as you pass again through Rottingdean stop a moment near the church. Here is left a small oasis: four or five of the prettiest eighteenth-century houses ever built round a duck-pond and village green, and just up the street the old Black Horse Inn which has not yet been chromium-plated.

It was in the bar of this inn that I met a very remarkable man. My over-friendly sheep-dog introduced us; the man patted her disgustingly fat flanks and said jokingly that I ought to be prosecuted by the R.S.P.C.A. for starving my dog. He was not a local, it appeared, but only down for a week. He seemed particularly bitter about ribbon development; it was just as bad up North where he came from; soon there would be nothing beautiful left in the world to see. The landlord, who had joined us, wondered if he would live to witness the final junction of Brighton and Rottingdean. They'd have to get a move on—he was seventy next birthday.

"I'd never have thought it," said the other man; "you've worn pretty well."

"So they tell me," answered the landlord. "But I don't deserve to. The old Boche made a proper muck of me in the last war."

The other man smiled and pointed to his face: "Well, you can see what they made of me."

I had not seen anything much—just that his eyes looked rather queer. I had not realised that he had walked over from that new concrete palace on the cliff—St. Dunstan's Hostel for the blind.

The coast from Rottingdean to Newhaven is probably the nastiest mess in the British Isles: first, Saltdean, an unplanned outcrop of concrete and gaudy red and green tiles; then Peacehaven, where bungalows like hen-coops, half-timbered

cinemas and garages, ye olde tea shoppes, and ye olde
smugglers' dens stand (or in some cases fall) between lines of
washing, notices of plots for sale, and avenues bearing import-
ant-sounding names. Each avenue is marked with its white
board. Each avenue has its asphalt surface for ten yards or
less, then becomes impassable to motor traffic.

If you pick on the right track (it is near Telscombe Cliffs
but difficult to find) you can escape from this Sussex war
memorial and reach Newhaven by a much longer but much
pleasanter way. Soon the track becomes many, each opinion-
ated as to the best way through the gorse bushes that crown
the ridge of down. But in winter don't stop to pick and choose
—keep the wheels moving or you will be bogged. All agree
in the end—they meet in the steep lane which twists down the
combe into the hamlet of Telscombe.

This hamlet is as secure from despoliation as any in Sussex.
In the first place it is doubtful whether the estate agents would
have discovered such a dead end—in fact, but for the racing
stables, Telscombe might have become as derelict as Ballsdean.   Now there is a further protection against building
or ruin ; bequeathed by Mr. Thornton Smith to the town of
Brighton, the village is in the hands of trustees.

There is only one way out of Telscombe : a single-track
road with views over the Ouse valley, and to Lewes, and to
the sea. It joins the Lewes-Newhaven road at Southease,
a hamlet lying off the main road and consisting of three or
four houses and a minute church. The church has a round
Norman tower of flint, capped with a wooden octagonal
steeple—a curious combination which exists in only two other
churches, St. Michael's of Lewes, and Piddinghoe. At first
sight the interior appears to be entirely primitive. The open
rafters, the simple wooden chancel arch, and the half-timbered
walls suggest a stable consecrated for some miracle in years
gone by. But it is not quite as unsophisticated as it appears.
Faint patches of fresco that have been lately uncovered prove
that the whole interior was at one time painted ; in the churchyard, foundations have been unearthed of two aisles and a
chancel (the present building being only the original nave).
The rustic wooden chancel arch is modern. As for the half-
timbering, I accuse it of being exposed.

It is seldom that I travel from Lewes to Newhaven ; when
I do, my goal is generally Dieppe : this road—twisting with
the twists of the Ouse—means that rather anxious thrill of
taking a car abroad, and every sharp bend spells boat fever.
I even find that, as I approach Newhaven, this landscape

begins to savour less and less of England and more of France :
the flat downs to the west might be the downs of Fécamp ;
and what could be more foreign than these little round church
towers fitted with their dunce's caps.

After Southease comes "Windy Piddinghoe," standing
on a knoll out of reach of the tidal Ouse. This is not England :
the tarry wharf, the jumble of orange-lichened roofs, the
strings of washing, and the golden weather-vane on the dunce's
cap—a fat dolphin nosing into the Channel gale.

Leaving Piddinghoe, you can see the derricks and cranes
of Newhaven harbour, and rows of blue slate roofs.   High on
the cliffs stands the parish church—another link with France ;
the Norman tower and apse are copied from the church of
Yainville-sur-Seine.   That is all that remains of the old
church.   The present nave is modern and dull.   There are no
fine monuments, but in the churchyard an obelisk brings back
the nearness of invasion during the Napoleonic crisis, when
the "grande armée" waited encamped outside Boulogne.
It is a memorial to Captain Hansen and a hundred and five
men who, during a storm in January 1800, were wrecked in
H.M.S. *Brazen*. The ship had been "ordered to protect this
part of the coast from the insolent attacks of the enemy."
Another reminder of recent history is the Bridge Inn, where
Louis Philippe (alias Mr. Smith) spent his first night in England
in 1854.

Otherwise the town of Newhaven holds little of interest
for the sightseer ; but the harbour has beauty—an unexpected
beauty—and, having handed over my car to the R.A.C., it is
in the harbour that I pass the three hours left on my hands.
I do not mean the dismal station and customs-houses that the
traveller knows, but the wooden wharfs and muddy creeks
on the opposite side.   There, against a background of tarred
sheds, fishing-nets hang festooned to dry, and in the creeks
are moored great rusty dredgers, and old packet-boats and
ex-royalties' yachts that have waited for years to be broken up.
The ebbing tide leaves derelict wooden hulks half swallowed
in mud.   And it is on this side of the water that sailors and
fishermen meet for their evening drink—in the bars you hear
the patois of Normandy, and get your first rank whiff of a
"Petit Bleu."

II

East of Newhaven the coast road follows the lowest spurs
of the downs to Seaford—a red-brick town of preparatory

schools. Just beyond the town a secondary road branches up the Cuckmere valley to Alfriston, a distance of three miles. Once a smuggler's track, it is now a tourist's way; for Alfriston is one of Sussex's professional beauties. During the summer season the ancient and mutilated market-cross is jammed round with motor coaches and cars. Half-timbering is responsible—black-and-white houses are needed to make a tourist's trophy village; in Alfriston the need is supplied by the George and Star Inns. In addition, there are some pretty weather-boarded cottages and, on the river bank, a fine cruciform church; but I can think of many other streets in Sussex — eighteenth-century streets — that have greater charm.

About the church, tourists have every right to complain. All that the interior can offer them are three sedilia, an Easter Sepulchre, a sixteenth-century bell, and some fragments of old stained glass; but, according to the Parish Guide, " the walls of the church were enriched with paintings which were disclosed in 1887 but were covered up again." The covering should be removed.

Ten minutes' walk beyond the river is a chapelry of Alfriston at Lullington. The church, which stands on a ridge of down within a sheltering circle of trees, " is much visited because of its very small dimensions," but it is under false pretences that Lullington claims to be the smallest church in Sussex. This is but a fragment; over a century ago the nave, a southern chapel, and part of the chancel were " quarried " away.

At Alfriston you can cross the river and rejoin the coast by the eastern bank, passing Litlington with its starch-white belfry, and the picturesque dead end of West Dean. This way you just miss the holiday camps and picnickers, and the Golden Galleon Café at Cuckmere Bridge; at last the downs are barren and for a moment it is possible to imagine the birth of this tarmac: the first footmarks of barbarians, a Roman causeway of oak sleepers, then the rutted track that served Saxons and Normans and remained much the same for centuries to come.

The minute church of Friston—the first building to relieve this ancient landscape—is not out of keeping. It stands, gale exposed, on the crest of the road with walls of chalky flints dating from pre-Conquest times. In a hurry you might think how charming, at the most peer through the door. That would be a mistake; for out of sight, in the north transept, is one of the pleasantest monuments to be found in Sussex. It is to the memory of Thomas Selwyn who died in 1613.

The composition is symmetrical; Selwyn and his wife kneel facing each other beneath an entablature of alabaster. Each is reading a Bible. Below, as a frieze, kneel their six identical daughters in ruffs and stomachers and farthingales. Between husband and wife, beneath the praying-stool, are laid neatly on a single cushion three pathetic babies in swaddling clothes.

If you have well-covered tyres, turn south at East Dean along the unmetalled track to Birling Gap. Birling is not only a gap in the chalk cliff but a gap in the defences of the private landowners; apart from the towns, this is the one spot on the coast where sweating holiday-makers can get into the sea, and in August the down turf is speckled with golfers, bivouacs, tents and cars. In the winter the sea mists seem bleaker as they shroud the empty hotel.

The road passes just below the crest of Beachy Head; if you can stand heights—but still enjoy the sensation of fear—walk across the turf and look over the sheer drop of three hundred feet on to the grey backs of seagulls that wheel below. But walk with care—the cliff overhangs to such an extent that you are on the brink before you know it. I have always considered it the most dangerous spot in Sussex, this unguarded chasm, which leaves coroners in doubt as to whether death falls are due to accident or *felo-de-se*.

Beyond Eastbourne (in which only the traffic lights should detain you) is a beach of shingle and coarse sand which is known as "The Crumbles." Historically this is the most important strip of beach in England, for it witnessed the last serious invasion of our shores when William, Duke of Normandy, landed in 1066. Apart from the bungalows (so favoured by homicides), and a continuous line of Martello towers—built to frustrate Napoleon's "grand army"—now derelict or converted into teashops, William's first view of Sussex must have looked much the same as now: to the west rose the chalk rampart of Beachy Head, to the east the Roman ramparts of Pevensey Castle—a ruin then as it is to-day. Anchored between these two landmarks rode the Norman fleet of some six hundred ships.

Except for seagulls wheeling in the haze of a September sky, the beach and marshes beyond showed not a sign of life, and William disembarked his army without opposition. The only mishap was that the Conqueror fell flat on his face as he jumped ashore—a mishap considered an evil omen by his troops until he wittily held up two handfuls of sand and cried, " See—I have seized England with both hands."

In fact, he made no further effort to do anything of the kind, but seems to have been as dilatory as our commanders at Gallipoli, who settled down to " dig in " on the beaches while the road to Constantinople lay open before them. Similarly, the gateway into the heart of England lay open for William : the high ground to the north-west of Hastings, which was then the only pass between the Pevensey marshes and the impenetrable forest of Anderida, was undefended ; the Saxon army under Harold was more than two hundred miles to the north fighting invaders from Norway.

William failed even to take the precaution of posting out-posts to protect this vital point ; for two weeks he did nothing except lay in some stocks of food, which he seized from Hastings ; hold religious services, for which he had brought over a large number of monks and priests ; and—optimisti-cally—burn his own ships.

In the meanwhile Harold—a brilliant general however unpleasant his character—was able to defeat the Norwegians at Stamford Bridge and, by forced marches, arrive in time to close the Hastings gap. William even allowed him to dig in across the pass ; if we take into consideration the type of armaments of the period, these deep ditches and sheer ramparts, reveted with stakes and hurdles, must have been as formidable as the Maginot Line.[1] No wonder the Saxon soldiers spent the eve of battle " carousing, gambolling, and dancing and singing "—while the Normans passed the night in prayer.

The battle that ensued should have proved a complete justification of Liddell Hart's theory of victory by defence. It opened at dawn on 14th October : a troubadour, Taillefer, rode at the head of the Norman attack, singing the songs of Roland and throwing high and catching his lance much as a drum major juggles with his mace to-day. Next came the standard—a holy banner that had been blessed by the Pope, and held concealed in the staff a hair from the head of St. Peter. Then followed the first wave of the attack : mounted on clumsy shire-horses and protected by tight-fitting chain armour, conical iron helmets and huge triangular shields, the Normans cantered ponderously up the long slope of wild, rough common into a barrage of javelins and stones—and

---

[1] There has been considerable controversy (Round v. Freeman) as to whether the Saxons kept to their trenches or defended themselves in closed ranks behind their shields. It is difficult to believe that a mere row of shields could have withstood repeated charges of heavily armoured cavalry.

retired. The few that penetrated, including the troubadour, were at once hacked down.

No other tactics could have better suited the Saxons ; by late afternoon their entrenched troops—though without even body armour—had suffered few casualties, while the attackers were almost a defeated army. Harold had everything to gain by waiting ; daily his command would have grown stronger while the enemy could receive neither reinforcements nor supplies ; had he been prepared to remain on the defensive —making no more than short raids from his trenches—the Normans must have eventually defeated themselves. As the day drew to a close, William began to realise how disastrous his tactics were proving, and as a last effort to force an issue he ordered a mock flight. The ruse succeeded : Harold, able general that he was, could not resist the temptation of a " decisive victory by force of arms " ; it was the same temptation that caused such appalling casualties in the last war and almost brought about England's defeat. He ordered the greater part of his men over the top.

" Out, out ! Holy Cross, God Almighty ! " The Saxons left their trenches, and the Battle of Hastings, which had dragged through a whole long day, was decided within an hour. Now each Norman arrow could find a mark, and their heavily armoured horses, hitherto so ineffective, proved deadly from their sheer weight and impetus. In the October twilight Harold found himself surrounded, fighting for his standard— almost alone. That he was killed by an arrow is a myth ; this is how an eye-witness described his end : " An armed man came in the throng of the battle and struck him on the ventaille of the helmet and beat him to the ground ; and as he sought to recover himself a knight beat him down again, striking him on the thick of the thigh down to the bone." At his death, the survivors of the Saxon army fled —even into the dread forest, or the marshes where many were drowned.

And so all England's destiny was changed by a tactical error in a miniature battle fought with clubs and axes, arrows and lances nearly nine hundred years ago—a tactical error that allowed " William the Bastard " to enter history as " William the Conqueror " ; an error so tragic that, to this day, the little Sussex streams run blood-red through the folds of the Weald.

> " Whose soil yet, when but
>   wet with any little rain,
> Does blush, as put in mind
>   of those there sadly slain."

III

Pevensey Castle stands theatrically among the marshes : huge crumbling Roman walls enclose eight acres of green. In the centre, insignificantly small in comparison, stands a mediæval moated castle. These outer Roman walls, which are five yards thick, are all that remain of Anderida, which, with Dover, Richborough and Reculver, formed England's front line of defence against the Saxons under the Roman " Count of the Saxon Shore." To-day these ruins make a welcome spot for charabanc loads to stretch their cramped limbs. But the marshes which lay to the north can have changed little ; here is an oasis of swamp where duck fly in from the sea to sleep within a circle of macadam roads. On winter evenings I have stood knee-deep in water while motorists' headlights flicked over my gun-barrel with the regularity of a revolving lighthouse beam.

Three miles of speedway raised above the flood-level, then the jumble of Bexhill, St. Leonard's, and West Hastings. There is nothing to distinguish one from the other except an unexpected patch of old-world cottages—the original Bexhill ; and, on the beach, the unexpected Pavilion of Chermayeff and Mendelssohn.

Hastings has two distinct sides to her character : more noticeable than in any other seaside resort (except perhaps Folkestone) is the sharp division between the bathing and fishing quarters of the town. The western quarter, as we have seen, is part and parcel of Bexhill and St. Leonard's. The eastern—a dead end below the cliffs—is something rare to find on the English coast : the little square of painted wooden houses ; the street of tarred sheds for drying nets ; the tarred boats and tarred windlasses on the silvery pebbled beach ; the jellied eel stalls, and lines of billowing shirts and pants ; all this has the same pictorial quality that brought Turner here to work—and the same romance that brought Rossetti and his tragic " Beata Beatrix " to be married in the parish church. But it is during the summer carnival that this dividing-line is most apparent ; they dance and drink in the streets of fishing Hastings—dance to tinny mouth-organs, with the top-heavy sheds and little painted houses a backcloth flickering under orange naphtha flares. In western Hastings there is acid flood-lighting : flood-lit swimming-pool, flood-lit Dagenham pipers, beauty queens, and *Daily Mirror* girls.

93   A Sussex Farmyard at Beddingham

94 Hurstmonceux Castle, Sussex

95   The Beach at Hastings

96 Fairfield Church on Romney Marsh, Kent

IV

I find Winchelsea as peaceful and pretty as any village on this coast. Peace it deserves ; during its first two hundred years of existence Winchelsea must have been the most unpleasant outpost of England. It was inundated in the thirteenth century when " three hundred houses and some churches were drowned." The town was then moved to higher ground only to be raped five times by the French between 1337 and 1440. And they came not just to conquer, but to burn and massacre, as reprisals for English excesses in France. On one occasion they surprised the whole town at Mass and none escaped. During the next century there descended the Black Death.

Even to-day—five centuries later—I experience some sort of fear as I climb the steep hill out of the Romney marshes and pass under the shattered gate. It is like returning to a ghastly trench in Flanders now grown green. However well tended the churchyard, however prim the white wooden houses that surround it like a cathedral close, there remain those empty arches, and this naveless, towerless fragment of the great church.

Even when peace came at last to Winchelsea, she came arm in arm with poverty : with the silting of the channel harbours the town lost all importance and there were no funds to restore the church—it remains to-day a partial ruin. But in these last years it has found a generous benefactor in Lord Blainsborough, who, as a memorial to his family, has presented an organ and filled the great windows with modern stained-glass by Strachan.

I came unprepared ; this is an art about which I am ignorant, and I had no guidance from intellectual or snobbish friends. I was in the position of the visitor to a modern art gallery who " knows what he likes "—but no more. True, I was judging only in comparison with such other stained glass as I had come across while writing this book : Burne-Jones, Kempe, Meyers of Munich, the Whalls, Rosenkranz, and Clayton and Bell. But it was not only through comparison that I came to the conclusion that these windows were the work of a very gifted and imaginative artist.

V

As we leave Winchelsea we see stretched below us a flat grass plain : the Romney marshes. Looking down from these last spurs of the Weald, you might well be standing on the

P

edge of cliffs overlooking the sea ; sidle down the cliff face
to the marsh-level and you will experience a queer sensation
that you are walking on an ocean bed ; it seems that these
isolated farms and churches have been inundated rather than
built on land reclaimed from the sea.   And this illusion is
made more real by these churches of the marshes—St. Mary's,
Brookland, Ivy Church, and Old Romney, whose interiors
are empty and stained with damp.   Most curious buildings,
with long double naves and no transepts, they are more like
barns than churches and are quite neglected : the walls lean,
the floors are broken (at Ivy Church it is said by horses'
hooves) ; but this dilapidation gives them a sad beauty, and
one is grateful to see the unrestored horse-box pews of bleached
pine, and, leading from the chancel, original Chippendale
gates.   There are seldom more than two buildings within
sight of these churches, and one wonders how their vast
interiors were ever filled ; but the minute church of Fairfield
seems to have less reason still, for it stands quite alone in the
middle of marshes, and looks like a toy dropped by a child.
Until quite recently, when a causeway was built, it could only be
reached during the winter on horseback (near the porch the old
mounting-block still stands).   When the bells were recast they
had to be ferried to dry land on a raft.   A service was held
only once a month, but Fairfield Church was sufficiently a
curiosity to have been restored—almost rebuilt.   The new interior is rather astonishing : dainty white horse-box pews and
a white three-decker pulpit under a raftered roof.

A few miles away is a poor relation, the equally small
church of East Guldeford, which also stands without a road
among the marshes.   Less isolated perhaps than Fairfield, it is
far lonelier ; few guide-books mention the building at all ;
Murray gives it under two lines : " In due time we pass the
still more miserable church of E. Guildford (*sic*) "—the less
miserable was at that time Fairfield.   It is only out of sentiment that I press some kind reader to waste a few minutes (he
must first find the key) and muddy his boots over Guldeford
Church.   Sentiment he will surely feel, and astonishment that
in England there should exist so derelict a building that
is still a church.   It stands among stagnant dykes ; grass
hides every grave.   Inside, the walls are fungus green, and
pale weeds grow from the cracked floor of the nave.   Recently
there has been a pathetic attempt to bring joy to this squalor :
a painted frieze of angels, in colour gaudy and crude.

At Brookland there is a curiosity (apart from the famous
twelfth-century lead font) that halts the passing holiday

97 The Overhead Bucket Line from the Kentish Coalfield to the Sea

98 Brookland Church on Romney Marsh, Kent

100 Detail of the Saxon Font at St. Martin's Church, Canterbury

99 Norman Door at Barfreston Church, Kent

crowds ; a comic wooden steeple stands on the ground some
distance from the church. Its reason is disputed, but it was
probably a matter of convenience—the marsh foundations
could not support the weight of a belfry, and the encircling
stream prevented an addition to the west end. In the inn
across the street other suggestions were forthcoming : the
landlord preferred the legend that, when an elderly virgin
came through the porch to be married, the belfry collapsed
in astonishment and was left where it fell. Others claimed
that it had been blown down by so many gales that the villagers
grew tired of putting it back. Another amusing theory is
that the architect, having insufficient space on his plan,
showed the belfry apart in the margin, and the builders
erected it accordingly—an ingenious solution this, except
that the belfry came three hundred years after the church.

Then the old verger—who was having his morning pint
—could stand it no longer : " These experts come along and
all says different. I know my version as parson used to tell
me and he came here over a hundred years ago." A challenge
came into his voice : " And I'm going to stick to it—they
wanted to use up the wood from St. Thomas' Forest, so they
decided to build a Norwegian Campanile." I was interested
—why Norwegian ? The Scandinavian influence on earliest
Gothic building is of course recognised, but this belfry
(and the similar detached steeple at Pembridge, Hereford-
shire) are more than influenced ; they are, to all intents and
purposes, copies of the pagoda construction of Norwegian
wood churches. Erected as late as the fourteenth century
they would, in fact, be an importation. The solution may be
that Scandinavian builders, recognised as masters of wood
construction, were invited over specially for this type of work.

The verger echoed another opinion of the old parson which is
worth considering : the piers of the nave here are splayed out at
such an angle that they appear in danger of collapse. I assumed
this to be the result of sinking. " Intentional, sir," corrected
the verger; " you have it in the Scriptures—' Build a house
for my children as an ark.' " Most of these marsh churches,
notably Lydd and Old Romney, have this same peculiarity. At
Lydd, certainly, the splaying appears too symmetrical to be
accidental.

VI

Though belonging to the marshes, Rye stands on a pinnacle—a last offshoot of the Weald. Like Pevensey the town

suffered centuries of rape and pestilence; like Pevensey it now exists on charm. But they are too picturesque, I feel, these narrow cobbled streets of ancient houses and antique shops over which two gilded cherubs strike each peaceful hour; and there are just too many water-colourists, perhaps, sketching the white windmill, and the barges with brown furled sails.

The coast road from Rye to Lydd runs wedged between holiday camps and chalets (all below sea-level) on the one side, and, on the other, the dyke that keeps back the sea. In summer it makes an entertaining journey: young things sun-bathing, elders asleep under newspapers, while every radio and gramophone is playing a different tune; but I once came this way in November—a sea mist was rolling in over the dyke like water in slow motion: in the purlieus of " Oakdene," " Home from Home," and " San Remo " I lost my way. The mist gave these chalets an exaggerated size; for an hour I wandered alone in what seemed a great empty town. Lewis Carroll might have imagined these nebulous palaces that shrank back again into dolls' houses every time I got out to ask my way. Looking through windows, I would see nothing but broken gramophone records, a paper parasol, and stacked deck-chairs. It grew darker, and I was beginning to wonder if a night alone here might not drive me insane, when, through a sudden thinning of the mists, loomed the square tower of Lydd Church —the Cathedral of the Marshes.

We pass New Romney Church, against whose walls the waves beat long ago (the marks can still be seen where ships moored), and Dymchurch with its fine Norman doorway; then, for the next five miles to Hythe, this fine modern road is protected from the sea by a wall that was built by the Romans.

The little town of Hythe clambers up the side of the downs to its formidable-looking church—formidable because the building has a most unusual construction: a high wall for a clerestory that reminded me of the fortified churches of the Dordogne. The interior, with its long flight of steps leading to the chancel and altar, is magnificent—one of the most impressive in Kent. The crypt holds a curious exhibit that many would like to see closed; here are some seven thousand skulls and bones of unknown origin. There are experts who put them as Celtic mixed with Roman, and even Lapp; others place them since the Conquest. No matter—I need hardly say that these relics draw a crowd; many, many tourists un-

interested in Ecclesiastical Architecture flock to pay sixpence
to view this gruesome pile of bones.

I should like to have spent longer in Hythe; it struck me
as being a very charming little town. I wish I could have
stayed to stroll under the elms on the banks of the Grand
Military Canal (which seems so pathetic a barrier to a Napoleonic invasion); and to have made a journey on the " Smallest
Railway in the World "—a miniature train which plies across
the marshes to Dungeness, between miniature stations and
signal-boxes all perfect in every detail. Above all, I would
have liked to have been here when the crypt was open—I
longed to see those skulls.

VII

England's twin harbours, Folkestone and Dover, are
separated only by the last narrow spur of the North Downs.
Except that they offer the shortest sea passage to France there
is little to be said for either town. In Folkestone the harbour
and old quarter have many picturesque corners and bars, a
palatial Edwardian hotel for those who cannot face a storm,
and a fish auction where I once bought (as a job lot) a live
lobster, a sole, and a little spiky goggling dragon for three
shillings and fivepence.

During a storm in 1702 the church was demolished except
for the choir. The nave and aisles were rebuilt and, during
the 'nineties, " enriched " with mosaics by Cappello and wall
paintings by Hemming. These works are lit by a huge west
window of Victorian stained glass—presented by three
thousand medical men as a memorial to the Folkestone
doctor, William Harvey, who, in the sixteenth century, discovered the circulation of the blood. It is certainly a rich
interior, but of the sort that I advise none to enter except to
pray. There is a small museum in the town which is said to
be interesting, but, with museum-like obstinacy, has always
been closed at such times as I have called. Some way outside
the town on the " East Cliff " are the foundations of a Roman
villa which became exposed during a fall of the cliff fifteen
years ago. Then, and during the excavations that followed,
considerable excitement was caused in the town, but that has
now died down; I had great difficulty in finding the site,
and my threepence admission was accepted with surprise.
It is all very neat and well kept : rectangles of rubble among
flower-beds and lawns, and, protected under a shed, a frag-

ment of a mosaic floor. Perhaps I was tired after our long
search ; maybe I was put off by my companion's flat refusal
to leave the car ; whichever it was, I found myself agreeing
with the guarded praise (or was it a warning ?) with which
an ice-cream vendor had pointed out the way : " Some *do*
say as 'ow it's quite interesting to them as understands."

The high road over the cliffs to Dover is bungalow strewn,
but a detour can be made—in fact, should be made—through
Capel le Ferne. The church stands in the middle of a corn-
field at the dead end of a rutted lane, and I should have never
troubled to discover it but for a charming acquaintance met
by chance a week or two before. He had come bustling into
a church just as I was about to leave ; a bearded little enthusi-
ast with determination far superior to my own : " Have you
found it ? Where is it ?—should be in the choir." I joined
in. Together we shifted pews and pulled aside carpets,
staggering like knockabout comedians under their rolled-up
weight. It was a long hunt, but successful—my new friend
stood aside : " Please proceed first . . . but, my dear sir,
I insist."

How could I escape ? I protested that I was in a hurry ;
I had left my materials at home ; in fact, with the idiocy of
human nature, I gave every excuse but the truth. And none
of them were successful. I was lent a sheet of foolscap and
a piece of heelball, and under those critical eyes I had to rub
a brass for the first time in my life. I am grateful to my
unknown friend, not for my clumsy rendering of a knight
and his lady (which, through childish pride, I still have not
destroyed), but for his insistence about this obscure church of
Capel le Ferne, and his foresight in describing where to find
the hidden key.

The interior, which is still lit by hanging paraffin lamps,
is unadorned and unrestored, and in the roof are the original
king-post and beams. But it is the Rood Screen with its ancient
primitive cross that makes this detour worth while—I have
only come across one other like it, at Westwell, seventeen
miles to the north-west. It is of stone, and a component part
of the church : three Early English arches and above them,
high in the roof, a rounded arch that holds the cross. It was
not alone the strangeness of this screen, nor its primitive
beauty that I found moving ; there was something else that
I could not define, something more than reverence, and more
than faith, about so costly and elaborate a structure of stone
pillars and arches built to enshrine a tumbledown wooden
cross.

101 Folkestone : the Old Town

102   Channel Crossing : the Dover Packet

103   Transatlantic Crossing : the *Caribou* at Rochester

VIII

As you drop down into Dover, the castle across the valley mounts higher and higher into the sky; with St. Mary's Church and the Roman lighthouse it makes a magnificent silhouette—as fine perhaps as Arundel—but I doubt whether a visit is worth the stiff climb entailed. The church of St. Mary's, perhaps the most ancient in all England, was used as a coal store until taken in hand by Sir Gilbert Scott. The exterior (which is presumably an exact restoration of the original) is very fine indeed. Of the ancient interior only two rounded arches of Roman brick survive. That they have no function is obvious—they can barely support themselves —but they have been left as curiosities. And most curious they appear in this setting of nineteenth-century mosaics which are the colour, pattern, and texture of bathroom linoleum.

The castle, which covers an area of nearly forty acres, was restored and remodelled in 1780. It has been used by the military for more than two thousand years : the Early Britons first fortified this natural rampart; the Romans made it impregnable with a *Castellum* of flint and brick; the idle Saxons profited—Dover was one of the few strongholds that the Northern invaders decided to leave alone. After the Conquest, the Normans added watch towers, a keep, and walls over seven yards thick, and thus changed our whole history. In 1216 Louis besieged Dover in vain; had it fallen, England to-day might have been a province of France, with open-air cafés, dinner jackets at weddings, gendarmes, and tolerable food. It was not until the Civil War that this fortress was taken—and even then it was not by force of arms : a Dover parliamentarian, Drake, climbed the sheer cliff from the sea, scaled the ramparts, and opened the gates to Cromwell's men.

A pageant of history has passed below these castle walls. They witnessed the final defeat of the Armada : all one Sunday our sentries looked down on a hundred and thirty galleons—close enough to hear the guttural lisp of a foreign tongue. All night they watched our flaming " fireships " drifting eastward—next morning, in panic, the great fleet had gone. It was from Dover that Henry VIII. set sail for the Field of the Cloth of Gold. Dover first welcomed Henrietta Maria as a bride—saw her depart again after she had said good-bye ; and to this same beach her son returned to claim the Stuart

throne. Twenty-eight years later William of Orange passed—
his fleet spreading across the whole Channel so that his men-of-
war saluted both French and English fortresses at the same
time. It was on these quays that Prince Albert disembarked
to leave London a memorial at least unique ; and the last
Emperor of France to find eternal rest in Farnborough
mausoleum. One more perhaps : a little moustached Frenchman wearing goggles, leggings and a sort of deerstalker's
hat ; but he landed on the turf above the cliffs—in a monoplane
—thirty years ago.

To-day Dover Castle is a barracks—and, for all I know,
still an impregnable fort as well—but it is such a medley of
restored mediæval walls, dried-up moats, out-of-date forts,
latrines, sightseers, and " Stop me and Buy One " merchants,
that it is almost impossible to know what's what.

The town of Dover is a very businesslike place—too
businesslike to have much appeal ; its only concern is to speed
the parting guest ; they do not, so a barmaid informed me,
cater for visitors. I tried every saloon bar on the harbour
without discovering a snack.

IX

Just beyond the castle a secondary road branches right
to St. Margaret-at-Cliffe, a pretty little bay with a Norman
tower squat enough to withstand every buffet from the sea.
Follow the hairpin bends down the cliff side and you'll find
the famous St. Margaret's Bay. It deserves its fame ; coming
there as I did during a heat wave between the Easter and
Whitsun holidays, I was almost persuaded to try again a
holiday by the sea. This little bay is imprisoned by two
ramparts of chalk that jut far out into the English Channel.
There are no golf courses in sight, and no bandstand or pier ;
but just a few yards of beach, a well-planned hotel with wide
verandas for every bedroom, two or three agreeable private
houses, a row of bathing-huts, and an old-fashioned inn with
a beer garden for " drinking Walmer's Famous Stouts and
Ales." And nothing to do but watch Channel steamers
passing, and charming young women in trousers exercising
Pekinese.

As we come into the town of Deal we pass two castles,
both built by Henry VIII. In each a famous soldier died ;
but one lives on in history. Walmer Castle, which is the
first we come to, is now the official home of the Lord Warden

104   St. Margaret-at-Cliffe, near Dover

105   Woodnesborough

Kentish Church Towers

106   Oast-houses near Sandwich, Kent

107 A Typical Kentish Yeoman's Farmhouse, near Sandwich

108   Broome Park, Kent : once Kitchener's home—now a hotel

109   Otford, Kent : once a Tudor palace—now a farm
labourer's cottage

of the Cinque Ports. It is open to the public on Thursdays. A guardian takes you through the gardens, which are magnificent, to the hideous little room where Wellington spent the last years of his life. It is a very good sixpence worth, offering just those intimate and gruesome details the sightseeing public demands : you are shown the "Iron Duke's" high writing-table (he always wrote standing up), and the iron camp-bed in which for four hours a night he slept (" Don't turn over in bed " was his maxim—" Turn out ") ; next the hard-backed chair in which he died, his death mask, and the handkerchief which held his jaw together after death.

The second castle has no relics—cannot even be visited. To discover some memory of the soldier who spent the last year of his life here as " Captain of Deal Castle," we must find our way to the hamlet of Ripple a mile or two inland. Here was the home of his boyhood, and here in the minute churchyard he now rests. His grave is inconspicuous—it has neither cross nor headstone, and I doubt whether I would have ever found it but for three wreaths of Flanders poppies left by the British Legion in memory of the Earl of Ypres.

Barham, though some miles from the coast, should be included, I think, in this chapter ; for here was the home of a third great soldier—at Broome Park. Let the history of this superb brick house lead us to the man ; it was built in 1638 (not, as most guide-books inform you, by Inigo Jones) for Sir Basil Dixwell, who signed the death-warrant of Charles I. Through his daughter and heiress it passed to the Oxenden family (one of whom—a murdered wife—haunts a bedroom to this day). For nearly three hundred years the building remained untouched except for the addition of an eighteenth-century drawing-room by Wyatt (*not* Adam) which is as pretty as can be. In 1861 Edward, Prince of Wales, wished to buy the house, but, with the owner Sir Montagu in a lunatic asylum, a sale was impossible—Edward bought Sandringham instead. After Sir Montagu's death the place was sold by his brother—and this is where our great soldier appears—it was bought by Kitchener. Broome Park was his home until he was drowned at sea, but never once did he sleep in the house ; he was too occupied pulling it to bits. He shortened the noble flight of steps that led to the entrance door, and over the door erected a porch ; he removed a Jacobean staircase and another by Wyatt ; he transformed the oak gallery into three small rooms, altered the levels of every floor, and added new carved ceilings ; in the living-rooms he built mantelpieces of marble, and on each he carved his motto : " THOROUGH."

Q

Then he was called to Russia, and a panel in the drawing-room bears only the charcoal sketch of a coat-of-arms which was never carved.

Now the fate of this house rests in the hands of a young married couple who, to save it from being pulled down, bought it to run as an hotel. They deserve success, for—in spite of the mutilation—there can be no pleasanter place in which to stay.

X

We will return to the coast across country direct to Sandwich; for between Deal and Sandwich there is nothing to see. As we leave the North Downs behind us, there occurs a conspicuous change in the countryside; it seems that, after three hundred miles of parkland, downland, and moorland, England has become suddenly bored with being English: this extreme eastern corner has the character, or rather lack of character, of the Netherlands. And to emphasise the change we even find houses from beyond the North Sea—seventeenth-century houses left by Flemish refugees from the Spanish wars; there are villages near Sandwich whose streets might have been painted by Pieter de Hoogh.

Another unexpected sight to be seen in this corner of Kent is an aerial ropeway that stretches east and west as far as the eye can see. For seven miles, two lines of buckets sway above the cornfields and copses—on one side returning empty, on the other carrying coal from the mines at Tilmanstone down to the harbour of Dover. As I passed these smoke-belching mines in their pastoral setting, I tried to put myself in the place of a miner—would I prefer to work here, or in the Black Country of the Midlands? To come to the surface on a summer evening and find gorse growing among the slag heaps; to go home to a cottage that backed on to a field of hay—that would be joyous. But to work all day in darkness under the roots, while above the corn is lengthening, the reaper clattering—what misery that would be!

So complicated is the network of small roads between Barham and Sandwich that to suggest a route would only ensure the reader losing his way. But Barfreston should be aimed at—the most ornate small Norman church in Kent, and Waldershare, that must surely boast the largest Baroque monument ever fitted into a family chapel. In fact, it can never have been fitted—the chapel must have been built specially

110 Old Farmhouse, Minster-in-Thanet, Kent

111 Cinque Port Architecture at Sandwich, Kent

112 Barn Interior, Minster-in-Thanet, Kent

round this alabaster group in which women and cherubs mount higher and higher until the last cherub almost hits his head on the beams. The monument is by a Thos. Green (perhaps a local man—there is a tablet to R. Green in the nave), and was erected to the memory of a tradesman, Sir Henry Furness, by his friends in 1732. His memory must have faded —these figures are now as mutilated as if they had seen the Reformation.

Lovers of Jane Austen should make a detour to take in Goodnestone Park—one of the few houses that the shy clergyman's daughter visited during her tranquil life. From her letters, these visits seem to have caused more pain of embarrassment than delight. As with us all (except the habitual house-party guest) her one concern was that dread moment when she must offer a haughty butler her humble tip.

Having come thus far out of our way, we might as well strike the Canterbury road and see Wingham and Ash. Had it not three stations, one would class Wingham as a village ; but town or village, the beauty of its solitary street and church can never be disputed. The church, with a needle-thin spire of copper, planted (more often than not at an angle) in the middle of a solid square tower, is typical of this part of Kent.[1] The interior is unattractive, for its stone piers have been replaced by baulks of chestnut wood ; but it contains two unexpected works of art : a fifteenth-century stone reredos from the French town of Troyes, and a copy of Leonardo's " Madonna of the Rocks," which must be a contemporary copy and, unless I am mistaken, in a carved frame of the same date. It is a remarkable painting and might even enter the lists as a third claimant in the National Gallery-Louvre dispute. In the Oxenden chapel is the family's most elaborate monument—white alabaster cherubs and flowers and fruit, held aloft by four black oxen.

I have two notes on Ash : in the church, a brass to the memory of Jane Kerriell, an entrancing little person whose " horseshoe " head-dress gives her the appearance of a Ming figurine. My second note is more personal : " John Coat, butcher, makes the finest brawn in England — *order more*."

Sandwich, the oldest of the Cinque Ports, has had a varied existence. A thousand years ago it was England's most important harbour. Though twice gutted by the French, it

[1] A curious variation is a cupola, sometimes enclosed by wooden rails (see Fig. 105).

continued to flourish until the annual customs approached
twenty thousand pounds. During the seventeenth century
the creek began to silt up and, though Flemish experts were
called in, Sandwich as a harbour functioned no more. Then,
in 1567, new prosperity came with the influx of Flemish
Protestants escaping the rapacity of the Duke of Alva—
" gentle and profitable strangers," who transformed the
marshes into England's first market gardens. The town's
position to-day is curious ; refugees we still see—no longer
Flemish, but Czech. Perhaps they, too, may introduce a new
industry ; as yet they do no more than wander through
the narrow sleepy streets uncertain whether to be grateful
for their escape from a concentration camp or bored to tears.
Not that Sandwich of to-day needs assistance ; silting sand
deprived her of prosperity, but this same sand has brought it
back ; these dunes, which at first sight seem to serve no purpose,
might have been deliberately designed by nature to add
irritation to the game of golf. The famous St. George's Club
is the most irritating golf course in all England, and therefore,
so it seems, the best.   To-day, tournaments and tourists keep
picturesque Sandwich thriving—look into any of the antique
shops and you can read the character of the town : among a
half-hearted display of Staffordshire and pewter ware, stand
bowls brimming with " pick ups " for resale at threepence to
sixpence a ball.

XI

A mile and a half from Sandwich, on a cliff in the marshes,
stand the ramparts of Richborough Castle—the Roman
Rutupiae—now left high and dry by the recession of the sea.
Seventeen centuries ago, with the sea foaming against its
walls, Rutupiae was Rome's Gibraltar which no barbarian
could pass ; and with its deep harbour and fine road, England's
chief port for all continental traffic. On the ramparts marched
in slow step sentries of the crack Second Legion—their eagles
and polished tin helmets garish against our solemn skies ;
on holidays, gladiators and athletes were cheered and booed
by the soldiery, while from the back, Britons peered agog.
Down in the harbour top-heavy triremes swayed with each
ripple ;   below deck, galley slaves slept or grumbled,
licking their sores. Closer inshore lay Rutupiae's famous
oyster - beds that supplied gourmets' tables in Imperial
Rome.

In time the great strength of this naval base became a

menace to the mother Empire; during the third century Carausius, who had been sent to protect the Channel from Saxon pirates, found it more profitable to intercept them *after* their raids. Ordered home, he made Rutupiae his head-quarters and set up as Emperor on his own. All attempts to dislodge him failed, and he ruled for ten years until murdered by his accomplice, Allectus. In the fourth century Magnus Maximus, given supreme power by his British Legions, used Rutupiae as a base for his attempted seizure of the Western Roman Empire—he took away with him his finest troops. Defeated in Northern Italy, they never returned—and for Britain this was the beginning of the end. During the next few years the great defensive general, Stilicho, succeeded in organising some of the remaining detachments against the waiting, watching Saxons, Scots and Picts. But this small distant island now seemed of very minor importance to the great Empire that was fighting to exhaustion against battering waves of invasion—a whole legion was withdrawn to defend Rome. In vain. Barbarians breaking through northern Gaul finally isolated Britain from all protection. Left without reinforcements—probably without news—this outpost of the Roman Empire carried on for another five years. Two Emperors were elected (and murdered) by the soldiers. Then a third, Constantine, organised an expedition to go to the aid of Rome. As with the previous expedition, the army was routed and never returned to these shores. But news did at last come from Rome, a message from the Emperor Honorus: in future England must fend for herself. The subsequent history of Rutupiae is a blackout; for many years, no doubt, these walls, which were three yards thick, were still regarded by invaders with respect; but it is clear that the lazy half-witted Britons made little use of what they had learnt from Rome. The fortress was plundered again and again, until finally, during the last century, the Kent County Council plundered the ruins to build their roads. To-day there is nothing to be seen above ground but three crumbled walls of elephant grey, and it is only in the museum that an imaginative mind can see some glimmering of the splendour of Rutupiae of Roman times: the fortress, harbour, naval base, barracks, shops, villas—all crowned by a colossal monument to the conquest of Britain, with pillars of white Italian marble and statues of gilt and bronze.

It was the humbler exhibits in this museum that I found most instructive: the various objects of everyday use. Con-sidering the animal existence of England's Middle Ages, it

seems incredible that a race could have experienced—a
thousand years previously—the state of civilised comfort
that these objects represent.   Experienced it and forgotten
it completely.   There is a show-case at Richborough with
needles and bodkins, jewellery, dice and gaming - boards,
hairpins and combs, crockery, cutlery, and every type of
glass, which might well be the counter of a chain store.

XII

Historically the coastline of Pegwell Bay is romantic—
almost every second name on the map is in Gothic type :
" The Monks' Wall," " Bloody Point," " Ebbstreet "—where
the Saxons first landed under Hengist and Horsa—and
" St. Augustine's Well," where a great Christian missionary
came to Anglia after Pope Gregory's famous pun.   This
scene must have been as fantastic as the descent of Victorian
missionaries on Central Africa : the Saxon king, with his
uncouth bodyguard, seated on the ground under an oak tree
(from fear of sorcery Ethelbert had insisted that the reception
should be out of doors) ;   the slow procession across the
marshes—forty monks chanting a litany and carrying primitive
ikons ;   and, at their head St. Augustine, a giant over seven
feet high, bearing his great silver cross.
    As we come in sight of Minster's steeple, our tyres must
cut the tracks of Domneva's hind which crossed forty-eight
ploughlands to found a monastery for " a multitude of
virgins."   In the eighth century Egbert became the fourth
Christian king of Kent by ordering the murder of his cousin
princess.   The crime was carried out by his devoted lieutenant,
Thunor, who buried the corpse beneath the throne.   From
then on a phosphorescent light glowed every night above
the grave.   In terror, Egbert confessed to Archbishop
Theodore and, on his advice, offered to pay " The Wergyld "
to Domneva, sister of the murdered woman.   She demanded
land to build a monastery—as much as a hind could traverse
in a single course.   In her presence, the animal was loosed
from the beach ;   straight across the marshes it sped as never
a hind had run before.   Too much for Thunor ;   surrepti-
tiously, he attempted to head the animal back to the sea, but
the ground opened and swallowed him at a place that is now
called Minster Chalkpit, but which is still known locally as
" Thunor's Leap."
    After Domneva's death, her daughter Mildred succeeded

113   Windmills at Outwood, near Reigate, Surrey

114   Weatherboarded Cottages at Cranbrook, Kent

115   The Water Front at Ramsgate

as Abbess. Burnt with all her nuns by the Danes, she became England's most famous saint, and her remains so valuable a relic that, when they were removed to Canterbury, the men of Thanet gave chase.

Finally, it may have been somewhere on this beach that Canute discovered that it is the moon that rules the tides.

Historically these are among the most interesting acres in England; but visually they are unromantic and dull. There are some traces left of the Abbey at Minster, now a private enterprise (admission 1s.); the church itself has fine Norman arches, and carved miserere seats, but an east window which prevents all enjoyment. Pegwell Bay has become a very snobbish suburb of plebeian Ramsgate. Ramsgate, on the other hand, has an unexpected charm. Once an insignificant herring-fishing village, it grew, during the eighteenth century, into a prosperous town " through the successful trade of its inhabitants with Russia." Later it became popular as a watering-place (according to *Murray's Handbook*, " slightly more aristocratic than Margate, though the difference is not considerable "). That was in 1892 ; but in appearance the sea front can have hardly changed. It rivals Weymouth in attraction, with its happy mixture of Regency and Victorian lodging-houses, small harbour, and rococo pleasure steamers fussing away from the pier. Apart from this old-fashioned appeal, apart from Pugin's Gothic home, the town has a characteristic almost unique in England : looking back from the quay it is hard to believe that this is not a continental seaside town—my photograph proves my point. I was puzzled—the architecture was English enough, and certainly the people. Why did this front remind me more of Dieppe—even Marseilles ? It was some time before I realised the cause : two restaurants with the audacity to flaunt open-air restaurant-balconies overlooking the sea.

Margate, like its more aristocratic neighbour, has seen little change since it first became popular, but I doubt if the town now claims to be aristocratic at all. That element must have moved to Cliftonville or Birchington-on-Sea, and there is a surprising lack of sophistication about London's most popular seaside resort. I had not been here since childhood, when recuperating from that mysterious Edwardian schoolboy complaint, " glands." I found that the promenade offered much the same amusements (though now, alas ! less amusing) as thirty years ago. The shell grotto, on the other hand, seemed more mysterious than before—as with

John Fuller's tomb, the mystery is that there should be a
mystery at all. Why has there " raged " (as Mr. Mitchell's
guide-book informs us) " a storm of discussion and controversy from which only a few clear facts emerge " ? How is
it that so many " theories as to its origin and purpose have
been advanced," some suggesting that this grotto is " a
Druid's Temple," " a Viking's Tomb," or " a Shrine of
Mithras," while others insist that it was made within the last
hundred years by a plasterer, or a schoolmaster, or " a travelled
cripple who had seen the Alhambra." How is it that Mr.
Harold Bayley in *The Lost Language of London* can write :
" I have elsewhere endeavoured to trace a connection between
prehistoric Candia or Crete and Cantium or Kent, and have
little doubt that the marvellous Serpentine shell mosaic
Grotto at Margate was built by Cretans " ? And Mr. J.
Malcolm Fraser, in *Pearson's Magazine* : " In the view I
have taken of the catacomb the age may roughly be
estimated at 2000 years " ? While Mr. Arthur Mee states :
" . . . purely the result of the astounding industry of an
English schoolmaster of the first half of the last century, and
with no great artistic or scientific significance."

Mr. Mitchell, who is proprietor of the caves, as well as
author of the guide-book, lectures the visitor with enjoyment.
He takes a strong line against any suggestion of modernity ;
on the whole he " is inclined to a Phœnician origin "—
but no other possibility is disregarded. The arches, for
instance, are Moorish, the Female Phallus (*sic*) is old Saxon ;
the Fan is Egyptian, the Marigold the " Sacred Flower of
the East " ; the " Tree of Life " comes from India, the god
Bacchus from Rome ; the absence of the emblem of the Cross
infers that the work is pre-Christian, the " Chapel, Shrine,
or Temple " is an exact replica of St. Botolph's in the
City.

In the end I decided to agree with Mr. Mitchell on one
point only, that " the work was never done in five minutes."
But whatever its origin, this grotto is as pretty as can be,
and a curiosity which deserves a visit : and I endorse every
one of the thirty-nine epithets which Mr. Mitchell prints
on his handbill : " Alluring, Archæological, Architectural,
Antiquarian, Astronomical, Bacchusgodical, Conchological,
Cruxansatical, Egyptological, Educational, Fulfotical, Ganesh-
godical, Geometrical, Geological, Holocryptical, Incompre-
hensible, Inconceivable, Inexplicable, Inexpressible, Inimitable,
Inscrutable, Magical, Mathematical, Mystical, Phallussignical,
Problematical, Shellmosaical, Symbolical, Symmetrical, Ser-

116 The De La Warr Tomb in Withyham Church, Sussex

117 Relief by Evesham on the base of the Tomb shown on Fig. 29, in Lynsted Church, Kent

118 Georgian Monument in Chilham Church, Kent

119 Reculver Church, Kent—as left by the parson

120 Herne Church, Kent: Ruskin's perfect tower

121 The Restoration Town Hall at Faversham, Kent

122 The Deserted Shell of the Jezreelite Temple at Rochester

123 Early Morning at Ickham, Kent

pentical, Subterranical, Sungodical, Unexplainable, Unbe-
lievable, Unfathomable, Unforgettable, Uranical, Whisper-
phonical, Zodiacal."

XIII

So flat and bedraggled is the country behind Margate that
one welcomes a foolish silver tower piercing the woods of
Quex Park. It houses the only peal of twelve bells in Kent.
Squire Powell Cotton had them cast to present to Birchington
Church in commemoration of Waterloo. The parish was
so slow in accepting that he built this belfry in his own
park. I should have liked to examine this "Folly," but
it proved unapproachable except by blatant trespassing in
full view of the house ; it had served a purpose, however,
in leading me to the "Powell Cotton Museum," which
otherwise I would have missed. Here indeed was a change
from this drab western landscape ; I passed through the
turnstile into the plains of Cashmere, the rocky pinnacles
of Tibet, the swamps and acacia trees of Central Africa, all
peopled with their stuffed denizens, victims of Major P. H. G.
Powell Cotton's rifle since the year 1895. Their realistic
arrangement and setting is miraculous—at first one is half
convinced that these are "tableaux vivants" rather than
"natures mortes." Almost every species of game, big and
small, is represented, including a record African elephant
with tusks weighing 372 lb., and the few gaps will be filled
before long : at the age of seventy-three Major Powell Cotton
has gone back to the jungle to shoot.

The twin towers of Reculver make another tourist's landmark ; they attract the usual crowd of holiday-makers who
will go out of their way to see a ruin. A hundred and fifty
years ago, when this church was complete, its curiosity value
was nil—to-day Reculver is properly supplied with car park,
postcards, and ice-creams. In a sense there is justification ;
for, as a parish church, the building can never have been as
impressive and romantic as it now appears in semi-ruin.
The pale primrose silhouette of the façade dominates the whole
flat landscape and brings crowds on the decks of ships passing
far out to sea. Not that this excuses the youthful Rev.
Nailor who, in 1809, with his Bishop's consent, began the
careful destruction of the ancient church in order to build
a new vicarage at Hoath, and an unpleasant Gothic Revival
chapel at Hilborough.

Leaving Reculver, we should be impressed by another

R

distant church tower, at Herne. According to Ruskin it is
one of the three perfect things in the world. Here Nicholas
Ridley preached, and in the nave stands one of those very
homely objects that can stir the imagination as vividly as
the finest narrative prose. Too vividly, when one thinks
of the calm courage and pride with which he sat back in this
simple oak chair while his congregation sang, for the first
time in history, the *Te Deum* in their beautiful native language.
How merciful that he could not foresee the full horror of
his punishment; for the burning of Bishop Ridley was most
clumsily done:

"But Dr. Ridley, from the ill-making of the fire . . .
so that the flames, which burned fiercely beneath, could
not well get to him, was put to such exquisite pain that he
desired them, for God's sake, to let the fire come unto him.
His brother-in-law hearing him, but not very well under-
standing . . . heaped fagots upon him, so that he quite
covered him. This made the fire burn so vehement beneath,
that it burned all his nether parts before it touched the upper,
and made him struggle under the fagots, and often desire
them to let the fire come unto him, saying, 'I cannot burn.'
In such pains he laboured till one of the standers by pulled
the fagots from above, and where Dr. Ridley saw the fire
flame up, he wrested himself to that side. At last the fire
touched the gunpowder, and he was seen to stir no more,
but burned on the other side, falling down at Mr. Latimer's
feet: his body being divided" (Foxe's *Book of Martyrs*).

XIV

It is best to avoid the road through Herne Bay and Whit-
stable (unless of course there is an R in the month), and go
direct to Faversham—a sleepy town on a sluggish creek.
Empty streets lead from the water to a market-square of
mediæval shops, white-washed town hall, and dark Georgian
inn. In the saloon bar, farmers talk on and on of the price
potatoes fetch per ton—and Lincoln is blamed for setting
a price too low. This town enjoys the combined somnolence
of an agricultural and bargee life; and two delicious types
of smell: down by the wharfs, mud and weeds and tar;
in the market-place, malty brewing beer.

The church interior is most ornate; the original Norman
arches were replaced in 1756 by a resplendent Georgian
Corinthian nave, which is generally deplored—though I

found it difficult to dislike. From the walls hang regimental banners, some faded and tattered, others brand new; there are a startling east window and painted reredos, over a hundred tombs, a varied collection of polished brasses, richly carved miserere seats, and a Baroque font. Among all this magnificence you may perhaps find the unobtrusive tomb of the English king who founded the original abbey. On the dissolution of the monasteries, two hundred years after his death, the king's grave was rifled for the lead of the coffin; his body was later fished out of Faversham creek and re-buried in the church. One can well imagine that after so long an interval the name of this king (whose reign had been one long feckless civil war) was, as it is to-day, no more than a schoolmaster's date. His tomb bears no effigy nor carved inscription—only a neat, non-committal, vicar-inscribed card: "In memory of King Stephen."

We join the Roman Watling Street at Ospringe—a village that must surely have been often named "The Venice of Kent." And it has as much right to the title as most of the other "Venices" outside Italy; a river has chosen to run between the houses. It is too shallow to be navigable, but calling tradesmen's vans must plough a watery furrow from door to door.

As you approach Sittingbourne, glimpses of a strange landscape appear between the houses: an unexpectedly desolate landscape of dark flats and marshes cut by two estuaries and endless creeks. It is the Isle of Sheppey, indeed an island of desolation which is emphasised by isolated factory chimneys and rows of cranes. Beyond the smoke of Sheerness lay anchored battleships—grey pyramids in a grey sea. It was in 1914 that I had last crossed the iron bascule bridge that joins this island to the mainland. I was a newly joined subaltern, on my way to Sheerness barracks. "Sheernasty" we called the place; and I remember my gratitude when, as a punishment, I was banished to guard some isolated fort on the mud flats of the Thames estuary. I have still a vivid picture of that little brick Napoleonic fort and solitary farmhouse which stood together and alone between weed-choked creeks and the sea; and a grateful memory of those few days' escape from barrack-square discipline and officers' mess romps. It was as a pilgrim that, twenty-five years later, I crossed once again the river Swale.

Except for its three new cinemas, Sheerness had not changed by one brick; and for this reason it now seemed a not unpleasant little town. The High Street with its un-

Tudored pubs, hideous Jubilee clock-tower, roving sailors and waiting girls, is like a coloured postcard from an Edwardian album. During the last quarter - century Sheerness has become a collectors' piece. Even the old Hippodrome (whose stage door was responsible for my banishment) still flaunts photographs of acrobats and ventriloquists in the face of Clark Gable and Myrna Loy.

As you cross the island—away from all factories—you find more than ever this impression of a lost, neglected land. The churchyard at Minster might be a fantasy of Edgar Allen Poe ; at one point it has been swallowed by a plague of ivy, which spreads from tomb to tomb, leaving dark poisonous caverns beneath. Inside the church, the walls are of rough stone and mortar and the monuments a network of idiots' names. For the antiquarian these monuments have a particular interest in that they show the development of armour during the last four hundred years. For the casual visitor there is a classic legend (which was put to verse by Bertram in his *Ingoldsby Legends*), a giant, and a dwarf. The legend concerns Sir Robert de Shurland, warden of the Cinque Ports during the reign of Edward I. His effigy lies under an elaborate canopy in the wall of the choir. Behind his head swims a horse. It is probable that this is a symbol of the knight's royal grant, " Wreck of the Sea," which allowed him to claim all flotsam he could touch with his lance after riding out within his horse's depth. But for centuries the local inhabitants have given a more enthralling explanation.

Sir Robert is said to have murdered a priest who refused to bury a corpse without payment in advance. Without evidence I suggest that Sir Robert was responsible for the corpse. But a priest was more dangerous ; in fear, he locked himself in his castle at Eastchurch, where he remained in safety for many months. Then, one morning, he saw from his window the royal barge coming slowly up the Thames estuary, and decided to swim out on his horse and beg for a royal pardon. This was granted by Edward on what he considered an impossible condition : Sir Robert must return the way he had come. No doubt Sir Robert had not been content with flotsam that was only within a horse's depth ; this horse proved to be a trained swimmer and did the double journey with ease. On the shore the knight was stopped by a witch who prophesied that this faithful animal would one day be the cause of his death—to defeat the prophecy Sir Robert killed it as it stood panting on the beach. A year

124   A Kentish Show Village : Chilham

125   Ospringe—the " Venice of Kent "

126   Early Morning at Wingham, Kent

127 The Marshes near Harty

128 Queen's Bridge

The Isle of Sheppey

129 A ruined Sheppey farmhouse : Leysdown, Kent

130 The Church at Minster-in-Sheppey, Kent

or so later, while walking on this same spot, he kicked against the half-buried skull, and a splintered bone pierced his foot. He died (presumably from tetanus) within a few hours. His last request was that the bones of his horse should be placed in his tomb.

The dwarf and the giant lie in contrast a few feet apart. The dwarf, Sir Thomas Cheyney, was about four foot six and quite bald. I know nothing of his history except that he was Sheriff of Kent and Treasurer to Henry VIII., but his character, mannerisms, even his thoughts are made clear by this alabaster effigy which is one of the most convincing portraits I know. Here is a dapper little dandy as self-conscious of his small stature and baldness as he was vain of his neat hands and feet and carefully curled beard. He was kind, though arrogant, with his inferiors—but a successful toady to the really great. He had wit, but would hold the table until he became a bore. With women he had the reputation of a lady killer—they all adored him—" he's such a pet." And that, in spite of the fact that he was fundamentally " queer."

The giant, Hugh Lord de Badlemere, was killed in the Wars of the Roses ; on his collar he wears the roses of York. He makes a moving picture lying in this complicated suit of armour that failed to save his life. Over his whole length of seven feet are carved the names of the Toms, Dicks, and Harrys of the last two hundred years. I had the patience to check the dates of these inscriptions—vandalism had continued unchecked since 1699.

Only when—still in vain search of my fort—I reached the extreme eastern coast of Sheppey, did I find some sign of more recent times. The shore had been transformed during these last twenty-five years—transformed in a most curious way : it seems that all the inhabitants have flown from this loneliness and these Siberian winds. Among kitchen gardens run wild, stand empty their well-built farmhouses just beginning to crumble into ruins. But in the place of these farmers a new tribe have settled beside the sea, drawn by a strip of sand, and their dwellings are surely as original as the tree dwellings of Central Africa or the pits of Neolithic times. There is a street of them at Leysdown—" Everowm," " Restawyle "—but such names are ironical ; for these dimity-curtained retreats are nothing more than old motor-buses ; they can never roam, must rest until the end of time—they have no " innards."

Behind these bus-bungalows lay only marshes—a green

baize cloth relieved by miniature windmills and the sailing shadows of fat cumulus clouds. They stretch south to Harty : an inn, a ferry, a church, and an unexpected tree. It was bad map-reading that brought me here. I suffered the irritation of five gates to be told that the ferry did not transport cars. And so I found in this church, which stands at the end of nowhere, a wood carving of two knights tilting ; a fourteenth-century muniment coffer ; a museum piece.

XV

Between Sittingbourne and Gillingham a narrow road follows the bank of the Medway estuary through Lower Halstow, where there are large brickworks and brick-laden barges moored in a smelly creek. We come to the village over a small hill. It would be rash to state that this is the most beautiful view on the coast—landscape-painting has taught me that such beauty depends too much on the light, the season, and one's momentary frame of mind. It is possible that I happened to pass at a time when this landscape looked its best : a soft drizzling afternoon in May. The sails of the barges hung dead—their damp ochre colour matching the wet piles of brick, the soggy reeds, and the desolate islands of marshland that lay in duplicate on the flat sea. In the distance I could see the thin outline of Sheerness, where every factory chimney held a rigid plume. The rest of this landscape was shrouded in a cloth of blossom, its whiteness unbroken by pretty mauve shadows, or any ripple of a breeze. Every object had sacrificed its identity to become a subdued note of colour woven into a background of luminous grey. But should the traveller come here at a time when sunlight and a blue sky make it all cheerful and commonplace ; or later in the year, when the blossom has fallen and the reeds are green — he will still find some compensation in Halstow Church, provided by an accident of the last war : heavy naval gunfire cracked the plaster font, which fell apart, revealing a more ancient carved lead font—a superb example of Byzantine iconography that some Puritan had covered up.

As you come into the outskirts of Gillingham, look closely for the most freakish building in Kent. Though planned to resemble the Heavenly Jerusalem described in the " Revelation," the building is now obscured by hoardings from the main road. The map shows it, and the name is enough to

131, 132   Modern Homes, Leysdown, Isle of Sheppey

133 Upper Stoke Church on the Isle of Grain, in the Medway Estuary, Kent

134   The Church at Wickhambreaux, Kent, seen across the Little Stour

135   Medway Barges at Rochester

encourage a search : " Jezreel's Temple." The building was
planned in 1885 by " God's last messenger to man," a soldier,
James White (*alias* James Jershon Jezreel), and his wife
" Queen Esther " (*née* Miss Clarissa Rogers). White claimed
to have received God's authority to gather together the
remaining one hundred and forty-four thousand descendants
of the twelve tribes of Israel, who, according to the Book of
Revelation, would escape death and be allowed to live on
earth with Christ for a thousand years before being taken to
heaven. Regiments of small children, dressed as angels,
canvassed through England ; candidates came from all over
the country—even from America ; cash poured in, but not
enough. This temple that was intended to reach up to heaven
had reached no higher than its third storey, when funds
ran out. It was as well, as the architect had forgotten to
allow for the stairs.

Rochester, though only thirty miles from London, is
almost inaccessible : the journey by road through South-East
London is a misery, and trains average one and a half hours.
One hundred and ten years ago the " Commodore " took
only four times as long to transport Pickwick, Tupman,
Winkle and Snodgrass, and " the green-coated stranger "
from the Golden Cross to the Bull Inn—and that in spite
of their frequent halts for " a glass of ale by way of
parenthesis."

The Bull Inn, the attractive street in which it stands, and
some exquisite eighteenth-century houses behind the Cathedral
are little changed except for an inscription over the hotel door
claiming " Good house—nice beds—*vide* Pickwick." And
the green-coated stranger's description of the ruined keep
remains apt to-day : " Frowning walls—tottering arches
—dark nooks—crumbling staircases." Not so the Cathedral,
whose walls are blackened by dockyard smoke and restored
by Sir Gilbert Scott. But the nave still remains one of the
loveliest in England—and, above all, a sanctuary from the
hubbub of armaments that goes on beyond the sound-proof
walls. For Dickens' Rochester has been strangled by its
neighbours, Gillingham, Chatham, Brompton, and Strood
—they are now one huge noisy town. I arrived in this turmoil
of bicyclists and lorries on a sweltering afternoon, and lost
my way. I was shuttled hither and thither by police guard-
ing dockyard gates, thwarted by one-way traffic streets. I
reached the Cathedral in no mood to write one sentence of
praise. First I found solace in a Catalpa tree, growing outside
the porch and in full snow-white bloom ; then I entered the

frigid calm of the great nave—cold grey stones that still held the dankness of Norman winters. A service had ended. The organist let linger a chill treble note.

But east of the choir screen all is not well: Sir Gilbert Scott had the misfortune to discover traces of heraldic paintings on the walls—golden lions on a red and blue ground. These lions are now repeated like a hotel wallpaper behind the stalls. True, Scott's intention was only to restore what he assumed to have been here before. His assumption may or may not have been correct—the result is hideously wrong. Cottingham's restoration of the superb Decorated doorway in the south transept is more successful—except for the head of a bishop placed inadvertently on top of a body in female clothing.

Excepting Canterbury, Rochester and London are the oldest Sees of the Church of England. The foundations of Rochester's first Saxon Cathedral were laid by King Ethelbert after his conversion to Christianity. The larger Norman Cathedral was begun by Gundulf, who built the " White Tower " of the Tower of London. But it was always the wooden bridge over the Medway—the link between the Richborough coast, Canterbury, and London—that had most effect on Rochester's history. For several hundred years the Cathedral was more important strategically than as a Holy See: then, after the murder of Thomas à Becket, the abbey became a roadside hostel where rich pilgrims passed the night.

During this latter period a most curious event occurred. That the monks had found it tantalising to see silver and gold and precious stones for ever passing eastward to enrich another cathedral—that is understandable. But whether they decided to rectify this grievance themselves or whether Divine Providence intervened—that the reader must decide for himself. Here are the facts: at the beginning of the thirteenth century a pilgrim—a Scots baker named William —passed the night in the Abbey. The next morning he was found murdered—without evidence or suspected motive his adopted son was accused. Now, there seems to have been little outstanding about the murdered man's character, except that he presented every tenth loaf he baked to the poor—a generous action, it is true, but surely insufficient to make a man a saint. Nor could one say that the unfortunate William had died a martyr's death. But a martyr he was proclaimed by the monks of Rochester; his body was buried in the Cathedral; miracles began to take place; some years

136, 137 Gravesend

138 Statue of General Gordon,
Gravesend

139 Trophied Gate Pier,
Petworth House

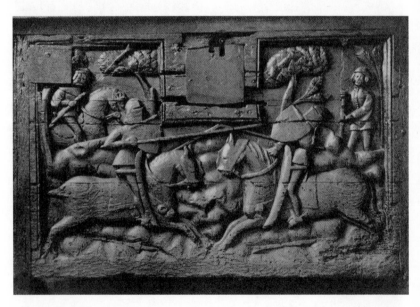

140 Mediæval Carved Chest, Harty Church, Isle of Sheppey

The Martial Manner

later William the Baker was canonised as Saint William of Perth; more and more pilgrims stopped at his shrine—and reached Canterbury the poorer. By the end of the century sufficient sums had been collected to build Rochester Cathedral as it stands to-day.

There now remain only a few square miles of this coast that are country—they lie between the Medway and the Thames. There is little except curiosity to justify a tour of this promontory; opposite Upnor, the Arethusa lies at permanent anchor—minute sailors perched like gulls on the rigging and spars; at Upper Stoke there is a pretty church interior of chalk; at Higham a pretty carved oak rood-screen; at Cooling an ancient castle gateway like a Victorian water-colour; on the Isle of Grain, an out-of-date brick fort that revived memories of a war game of my childhood: "Attack." But the most curious aspect of this last stretch of coastline is that it has not yet been "developed." Here, almost within sight of London's tentacles, the growing of food has remained more important than bungalow life. Every acre is cultivated—acres of grass, acres of wheat, and, above all, acres of potatoes. There are no hedges to separate the fields, few trees to waste the land. Only an occasional poplar breaks the skyline and emphasises the astonishing resemblance that this landscape bears to the plains of Northern France.

T

XI

HOMEWARD JOURNEY

I

ON the spur of the moment I decided to return by train. It was a journey of curiosity rather than convenience— a curiosity that had been aroused during the past winter. I had been attending Territorial drills in Brighton and, when the nights were foggy or too cold for words, I used to catch the 5.14 from Uckfield rather than face the double journey by road. It was most important that the train should be reasonably punctual, for if she was more than twenty minutes behind time it meant my being late on parade. But whenever I started pestering my friend the stationmaster. he would rebuke me: "There's no telling, sir, when she'll be in—you see, she comes all the way from Chatham, and there's snow on the line." Back I would go to the warmth of the Railway Hotel, where, fortunately, the landlord had ears tuned to the shutting of the level-crossing gates. In time the stationmaster's attitude became infectious; I no longer regarded this train as a mere unpunctual nuisance. When the gates at last clanged to, and the engine's lights appeared round the Buxted curve, this 5.14 from Chatham seemed to me every bit as romantic as the trans-European expresses that pull into the Gare de Lyon, their *wagon-lits* heavy with steaming snow and bearing the names of far-distant capitals.

Never again, I felt, would I find myself in Chatham; this was my opportunity to experience that adventurous journey through the Weald of Kent. I left my car to make its own way home under the doubtful guidance of a friend.

As an adventure the journey fell flat—but that was to be expected; it was impossible even to imagine those wintry evenings on this burnished summer afternoon. And the time passed quickly—all too quickly; in under two hours I had retraced my travels of many weeks. But as an experience, this journey was enlightening, for I found that in all those weeks of travel I had still missed the peaceful beauty of Kent.

Almost the whole way the line follows the valley of the Medway: at Rochester an estuary as wide as an arm of the sea, with trans-Atlantic planes riding at anchor beneath the walls of the keep. At Snodland (which must surely have suggested to Dickens his name for Pickwick's friend), the river narrows to cut through the chalk-ridge of the North Downs, and cement works line the banks, powdering a dirty white all grass and trees. But above Maidstone industrialism ends, and the folds of the Weald enclose a tranquil stream-course that for many miles can be reached only by tracks, and only crossed by mediæval bridges of lichened stone.

Softly the woods slope down to overhang the placid flow —soft as the cloud shadows drifting leisurely among the quilted fields. Softly our white smoke melted into blue, while pigeon rose from the full-grown corn. The orchards were heavy, and the hops had spread their tentacles as far as they could grow. Fishermen sat watching the wavering movement of their floats, or lay sprawled, leaving their rods to care for themselves. Never have I looked upon a landscape so unperturbed.

Before very long now, clattering reapers would leave avenues of gold . . . cockney invaders would strip the hops. Before long there would come " a chill in the air " . . . the " nights would draw in " . . . a jaundiced leaf would flutter to break the reflected pattern of a leaden sky. Then how quickly would winter come! . . . " She's all the way from Chatham, sir " . . . Two pin-pricks of light on the Buxted curve. The 5.14—so proud of her sprinkling of snow.

It *was* 5.14—to the minute: the level-crossing gates were closed and the two lines of cars stretched up either hill. Those children raced up the steps on to the bridge to spit before we passed. " UCKFIELD "—" UCKFIELD "—my home town.

II

Now that I have reached the end of this book, I realise how reticent I have been about this home town of mine—so reticent as to arouse suspicion: a photograph of a fair ground, that is my only reference. Suspicion is justified;

I must confess that I have been trying to shirk an unpleasant duty, for there is little that I can say in praise. Not that Uckfield is altogether unsightly; above the cross-roads, where the policeman stands on point duty, all the houses are attractive, some even beautiful. But travellers from London shoot past (and don't slow up until the policeman comes in view); those from Eastbourne have already seen the High Street, with its cinema, drill hall, chapel, station, and the railway hotel—and seen enough. Even when they do stop for a drink, they just troop into the bar of the " Maiden's Head " and out again, without noticing the superb Georgian façade. Poor Uckfield, she is as neglected as a woman, comely above the waist but with bad legs—legs so gross and misshapen that no man ever takes the trouble to turn and look at the face. Quite soon—if the builders have their way—she'll have no looks left at all. But I shall love her just the same.

Rereading these last lines, I realise how inconsistent they must seem, when throughout this book I have never failed to ridicule the newborn ugliness of almost every town and village I have seen. About Uckfield I must have a beam in my eye—and no doubt every average Englishman is similarly half blind when he looks at his own home. For we have carried our insularity within far narrower limits than our shores, and become so complacent that we can dispense with beauty altogether; we regard her to-day as a purely foreign product—a curiosity, quite enjoyable in the right place, but necessitating a trip to Venice or, failing that, room must be found on the mantelpiece for a coloured photograph of the Taj Mahal. As regards his own surroundings the average Englishman seems to have decided what he wants—architects with new ideas (they, too, are regarded as alien) had better try them out elsewhere; " Societies for the prevention . . ." have not the slightest hope of preventing anything at all. One cannot blame the average Englishman; he has had to fight for centuries to make his country how he likes it. Soon he will have to fight again to keep it as it is—so sandbag our Tudoresque bungalows, while St. Paul's falls down !

Maybe that will prove our only strength.

INDEX

(The numerals in heavy type denote the *figure numbers* of illustrations)

117